Istanbul is a chaotic, bustling, tra
commit into words or fully unde
personality spans its gigantic geo
many diverse neighbourhoods w
imperfect beauty in every corner
and untamed soul is evident in its _____ _____ cuisine,
ever-impressing with creative flavours, turning visitors into addicts
and in some instances expats. Set out of the Old City and into the
many faces of the city to get a sense of its true nature.

CITIx60: Istanbul explores the art-rich Turkish capital through the
eyes of 60 stars from the city's creative scene. Together, they
take you on a journey through the best in architecture, art spaces,
shopping, cuisine and entertainment. This guide will lead you on an
authentic tour of Istanbul that gets to the heart of what locals love
most about their city.

Contents

Before You Go

BASIC INFO

Currency
Turkish Lira (TRY/TL)
Exchange rate: US$1 : 2.9 TL / €1 : 3.2 TL

Time zone
GMT +2
DST +3

DST begins at 0200 (local time) on the last Sunday of March and ends at 0300 (local time) on the last Sunday of October.

Dialling
International calling +90
Citywide (0)212/216*

*Dial (0) for calls made outside Istanbul within Turkey.

Weather (avg. temperature range)
Spring (Mar–May): 4–21°C / 39–70°F
Summer (Jun–Aug): 16–29°C / 61–84°F
Autumn (Sep–Nov): 9–25°C / 48–77°F
Winter (Dec–Feb): 3–11°C /37–52°F

USEFUL WEBSITES

Bus routes and journey planner
www.iett.gov.tr

EMERGENCY CALLS

Ambulance
112

Police
155

Fire
110

Consulates
China   +90 212 299 2188
France   +90 212 334 8730
Germany   +90 212 334 6100
Russia   +90 212 292 5101
UK   +90 212 334 6400
US   +90 212 335 9000

AIRPORT EXPRESS TRANSFER

Atatürk Havalimanı <-> Taksim (Metro M1A > M2)
Train / Journey: every 5-7 mins / 35 mins
From Havalimanı (M1A) – 0600–0000
From Taksim (M2) – 0619–0020
(Change at Yenikapi)
One-way: 4 TL (Token) / 2.15 TL (Akbil, Istanbulkart)
www.istanbul-ulasim.com.tr

Sabiha Gökçen Airport <-> Taksim (Havataş bus)
Bus / Journey: every 30 mins / 90 mins
From Sabiha Gökçen Airport – 0400–0100
From Taksim – 0330–0100
One-way: 14 TL
www.havatas.com

PUBLIC TRANSPORT IN ISTANBUL

Bus
Tram
Metro/ funicular subway
Light rail
Ferry
Taxi

Means of Payment
Istanbulkart
Credit cards
Cash

PUBLIC HOLIDAYS

January	1 New Year's Day
April	23 National Sovereignty & Children's Day
May	1 Labour & Solidarity Day, 19 Commemoration of Atatürk, Youth and Sports Day
June/July	Ramadan (3 days)*
August	30 Victory Day
September	Sacrifice Feast (4–5 days)*
October	6 Liberation of Istanbul, 28 Republic Day (1.5 days)

On the first days of religious holidays*, which drift around 11 days earlier each succeeding year, shops and attractions open at 1pm where cultural institutions are closed. Bazaars are likely closed all Sundays and public holidays.

FESTIVALS / EVENTS

February
!f Film Festival (also in March)
www.ifistanbul.com

April
Istanbul International Film Festival
film.iksv.org
Tulip Festival

May
Istanbul International Music Festival
muzik.iksv.org
Istanbul International Theatre Festival
tiyatro.iksv.org
Istanbul International Arts & Culture Festival
(also in June)
istanbul74.com/festival

July
Istanbul International Jazz Festival
caz.iksv.org

September
Istanbul Biennial (next edition happens in 2017)
14b.iksv.org
Akbank Jazz Festival
www.akbanksanat.com

October
Istanbul Design Biennial (next edition happens
in 2016)
tasarimbienali.iksv.org
Istanbul Coffee Festival
www.istanbulcoffeefestival.com

November
Contemporary Istanbul
contemporaryistanbul.com
Istanbul Book Fair
www.istanbulkitapfuari.com
Istanbul Light Festival
istanbullightfestival.com

Event days vary by year. Please check for
updates online.

UNUSUAL OUTINGS

Artwalk Istanbul
www.artwalkistanbul.com

Street art, mushroom hunt, coffee workshop
istanbultourstudio.com

Custom-designed tours by Serhan Güngör
www.serhangungor.com
www.festtravel.com

Istanbul Photography Tour
www.istanbulphotoworkshops.com

The Other Tour
theothertour.com

SMARTPHONE APP

Public transport routes & traffic conditions
TRAFI Public Transport

Cycling routes, repair stations &
Bisikletli Ulaşım Haritası (TR)

REGULAR EXPENSES

Domestic letters / international airmail
1.4 – 2.8 TL

Turkish coffee
5–10 TL

Bike rental
5–10 TL per hour

Gratuities
Diners: 5–10% for waitstaff & bartenders
Hotels: 5 TL for porters and 5–10 TL daily for
cleaners
Licensed taxis: Round up to the nearest Lira
Turkish baths: 10–20% for attendants

Count to 10

What makes Istanbul so special?
Illustrations by Guillaume Kashima aka Funny Fun

Istanbul offers a perfect balance of the past and the future, with contemporary art showcased in historic buildings, age-old recipes reinvented in contemporary kitchens, and traditional motifs resurfacing as modern designs, making this adorably chaotic city a trove of creativity and innovation. Whether you are here for a day or a week, see what Istanbul's creative class consider an essential to-do list.

İSTANBUL'A HOŞ GELDİNİZ

SELFIE @ THE ŞAKİRİN MOSQUE

1

Architecture

Kamondo Stairs
Karaköy, Bankalar Cad., Beyoğlu

Şakirin Camii
by Hüsrev Tayla & Zeynep Fadıllıoğlu

Sancaklar Camii
by Emre Arolat Architects

Botter Apartment
by Raimondo D'Aronco

Atatürk Kültür Merkezi (#1)
by Hayati Tabanlıoğlu

Haydarpaşa Garı (#2)
by Otto Ritter & Helmuth Conu

İstanbul Deniz Müzesi
by Teğet

Kuzguncuk (Üsküdar), Balat (#5)
Old localities with multiethnic traces

Besiktas Balıkcılar Çarşısı
by GAD

5   6   7

Turkish Bath

Kilic Ali Pasa Hamamı
Beautifully updated Sinan design
with gender-specific bathing hours
kilicalipasahamami.com

Ayasofya Hürrem Sultan Hamamı
Carefully restored Sinan design
matched with fine bath accessories
www.ayasofyahamami.com

Çemberlitaş Hamamı
Faithfully reserved Sinan design,
runs daily from 6am to midnight
www.cemberlitashamami.com

Çağaloğlu Hamamı
Twin hamam with a long tradition
www.cagalogluhamami.com.tr

...

Peştemal (hamman towel)
Abdulla @Grand Bazaar (#31)
Beşiktaş Cumartesi Pazarı
(Saturday Market)

Local Staples

Turkish coffee
Mandabatmaz (#48)

Meze & rakı
Sehir Meyhanesi (*Galatasaray*)
Meze By Lemon Tree (*Şişhane*)
Karaköy Lokantası (*Karaköy*)
Cibalikapı Balıkçısı (*Moda*)

Kebab & Ayran (salted yogurt drink)
Çiya Sofrası (#37)
Umut Ocakbaşı, *umutocakbasi.com.tr*
Köşebaşı, *www.kosebasi.com*

Mantı (Turkish dumplings)
Yeni Lokanta, *lokantayeni.com*

Midye Dolma (stuffed mussels)
İstiklal Cad., *Beyoğlu*

Grilled lüfer (blue fish)
Balıkçı Sabahattin (*Sultanahmet*)
Kiyi, *www.kiyi.com.tr*
Adem Baba, *www.adembaba.com*

Sugar Fix

Baklava (nut-filled filo pastry)
Karaköy Güllüoğlu (*Karaköy*)
Pare Baklava Bar (*Nişantaşı*)

Lokum (Turkish delight)
Ali Muhiddin Hacı Bekir (*Taksim*)
Cafer Erol (*Karaköy*)
Lokum Istanbul (*Arnavutköy*)

**Dondurmalı irmik helvası
(ice-cream stuffed
Semolina-based halva)**
Hünkar (*Nişantaşı*)

Katmer (fried layered bread)
Zerafet (*Beşiktaş*)
Develi (*Fenerbahçe*)

Aşure (dessert congee)
ZerafEt (*Ulus*)
Göreme Muhallebicisi (*Nişantaşı*)

**Mesir macunu
(sweet paste made from 41 herbs)**
Misir Carsisi (*Eminönü*)

8
Pazarı
(markets)

Kapalı Çarşı (Grand Bazaar)
*Scarfs @Yazmacı Murat, vinyls
@Gramofon Baba, lahmacun @Burç
Kebap, textile @Dervis*

Misir Carsisi (Egyptian Spice Bazaar)
*Freshly ground Mehmet Efendi
coffee, fruits and nuts, spices, olives
& essences of the finest order*

Feriköy Bit Pazarı (Flea market)
*Antiques on Sundays &
organic goods on Saturdays*

**Fatih Çarşamba Pazarı
(Wednesday Market)**
Fresh produce & household items

Kasımpaşa İnebolu Pazarı
*Chefs' favourite Sunday market for
fresh produce from İnebolu*

Karaköy Perşembe Pazarı
*Thursday market woodworking
equipment & precision tools*

9
Tattooists

Okan Uçkun
www.okanuckun.com

Bicem Sinik
instagram: @bicemsinik

Emrah Ozhan
instagram: @emrahozhan

Resul Odabas
instagram: @resulodabas

Red Cat Tattoo Factory
www.redcattattoo.com

10
Mementos

Calligraphic prints
Nick's calligraphy @Grand Bazaar

**Çini (traditional Turkish
pottery) & ceramics**
Iznik art @Grand Bazaar

**Traditional kilim (tapestry-woven
carpets) or pillowcases**
*Recep Karaduman, Dhoku,
Sişko osman @Grand Bazaar*

Turkish coffee
*Kurukahveci Mehmet Efendi
@Misir Carsisi*

Turkish music instruments
*Galip Dede Cad., Tünel
Handmade Cymbals: İstanbul
Mehmet, www.istanbulmehmet.com*

Modernised tea glasses
*Paşabahçe
www.pasabahce.com*

Icon Index

 Opening hours

 Admission

 Address

 Facebook

 Contact

 Website

 Remarks

 Scan QR codes to access Google Maps and discover the area around each destination. Internet connection required.

60x60

60 Local Creatives x 60 Hotspots

From vast cityscapes to the tiniest glimpses of everyday exchange, there is much to provoke one's imagination. 60x60 points you to 60 haunts where 60 arbiters of taste develop their good taste.

Landmarks & Architecture
SPOTS · 01 – 12

Immerse yourself in Istanbul's history through its magnificent architecture. Experience the city's wonders by boat or walk, and make sure you have your camera with you.

Cultural & Art Spaces
SPOTS · 13 – 24

Get on board with the contemporary art scene and tour the galleries, old and new, to witness first-hand the flourishing creations of Istanbulites.

Markets & Shops
SPOTS · 25 – 36

Once you've completed your to-do list, let your impulses lead the way as you visit vintage stores, flea markets, and concept stores.

Restaurants & Cafés
SPOTS · 37 – 48

Any trip to Istanbul is an absolute foodie adventure with a varied cuisine that never ceases to amaze. Make sure you indulge in age-old recipes and desserts as much as their new cuisine.

Nightlife
SPOTS · 49 – 60

Whether you plan for a wild night or not, Istanbul's after-dark scene offers plenty, from live gigs and local bars to posh clubs and electro nights.

Landmarks & Architecture

Ottoman houses, modern architecture and Byzantine influences

Istanbul's complex history can be understood through its architecture filled with Byzantine, Ottoman, and contemporary era structures that side by side create a landscape that flawlessly merges the past lives of the city. Some of the oldest and most extravagant examples are naturally found in the Old City, with Hagia Sophia (#8) dominating the Sultanahmet Square and the Sunken Palace (#9) imposing its grandeur underground.

The city is home to many mosques and some of the more modern ones (listed under *Count to 10*) are worth visiting to get a glimpse of the true reincarnation of faith through design. Other modern architectural marvels are spread around the city, like Kanyon (#11) with its award-winning design, and Zorlu Center, a superimposed structure by Emre Arolat Architects and Tabanlıoğlu Architects in Levent.

A boat tour is highly recommended not only to get a cool breeze but to take in the wonderful architecture of *yalı* (waterfront mansions) that line both sides of the Bosphorus, like the Perili Köşk (#3).

Italian, German, and Armenian architecture is evident in older neighbourhoods like Balat (#5), Galata (#29), Karaköy and Çukurcuma (#34). Grab your camera and a pair of comfortable walking shoes, and get lost amongst the grandeur of 19th and 20th century designs.

Berent Baytekin
Founder, Autonomy

Creative director and producer Berent Baytekin has been in the Turkish film industry for more than 20 years. He has produced short films, music videos and more than 600 commercials.

Haydarpaşa
Garı
P.015

Turgut Akaçık
Film director, Autonomy

I direct commercials at Autonomy. I like kitesurfing, riding my motorcycle and spending time with my pets when I am free.

Can Büyükberber
Visual artist & director

I focus on digital art, motion graphics and audiovisual performance. I'm obtaining a Master's in art and technology and working on immersive experiences with sound, light and space.

Atatürk
Kültür
Merkezi
P.014

Perili Köşk
P.016

Ayşegül Akçay Kavakoğlu
Architect, researcher & educator

I'm curious about the ways of design and imagination, and am addicted to finding out about the relationship between moving image and design. I teach at İstanbul Kemerburgaz University.

Balat
P.020

Murat Beşer
Music journalist & DJ

I create content on music and pop culture for print and broadcast media including Stüdyo İmge, Cumhuriyet and TRT. I'm an advisory board member of the Istanbul Jazz Festival.

Halit Fatih Kızılgök
Film director

I studied liberal arts and experimental cinema in the US. An European Film Academy nominee for *Dust*, I direct commercials, short films and am writing ideas down for a feature film.

Galata Kulesi
P.017

Galata
Köprüsü
P.022

Volkan Dede
Film director, Walky–Talky

I'm a commercial director, sociology graduate, PhD dropout and father of one sweet cherry. I'm one half of director duo Walky–Talky.

Ayasofya
P.024

Meltem Özbek
Fashion designer

I love asymmetric shapes and using leather or suede for my clothing and bag collections. My inspirations include architecture and nature.

Aykut Aydoğdu
Illustrator

I worked as an art director after graduating from graphic design at Hacettepe University, but later couldn't resist my passion for drawing and went on to pursue my beloved craft.

Maçka
Demokrasi
Parkı
P.023

Yerebatan
Sarayı
P.026

Aslı Filinta
Fashion designer

I created my namesake label in 2008 after graduating from Parsons New York. My design is characterised by unexpected combinations of materials and its balance of light and delicate fabrics.

Kanyon
P.028

Tamer Nakışçı
Founder, Futureisblank

My experience spans technology, multi-sensorial installations, automotive and product design. My work focuses on the interactions between people, spaces and objects.

Volkan Yıldırmaz
Painter & sculptor

I'm Volkan, English for volcano. The dynamics of Istanbul is the engine to my work. The city evolved as frequently as my haircuts and I adore the brutal lifestyle of the streets and people.

Süleymaniye
Camii
P.027

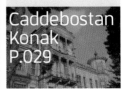

Caddebostan
Konak
P.029

1 Atatürk Kültür Merkezi
Map D, P.106

Named after Mustafa Kemal Atatürk (1881–1938), the founder of the Republic of Turkey, Atatürk Cultural Centre, or simply AKM, stands as an architectural and cultural reference point at the heart of Taksim Square. Once the grand stage for state-funded performing arts, up until 2008 when it was closed infinitely for the long overdue renovation works, AKM is now a rallying point for security forces at time of protests and the pivot of continual political infighting over the centre's future. The best time to view this modernist giant is now as it's at risk of being razed or replaced. The steel façade was conceived by Tabanlıoğlu Architects in 1977, who is also behind Istanbul Modern's design.

🏠 *Gümüşsuyu, Tak-ı Zafer Cad., Beyoğlu*

"To many, bringing down AKM means demolishing modern Turkey. The giant matchbox might not be here on your next visit. Take as many photos as you can!"

– Berent Baytekin, Autonomy

2 Haydarpaşa Garı
Map J, P.109

Having survived multiple fire and blasts, the neoclassical Haydarpaşa Terminal still stands in its glory by the Bosphorus. Before its temporary closure in 2012, the U-shape German design was the first stop of the Istanbul-Baghdad railway and a symbol of the close Turkish-German relations at the time of construction in 1908. Plans to repurpose the terminus were much disputed and its lucky escape means that future restoration work will see the return of its grandeur, and its original function as a train station. The time frame to reopen is uncertain but visitors can still enter the building and chill at the Turkish tavern inside.

🏠 Rasimpaşa, Haydarpaşa Garı, Kadıköy

"If you don't have time for a visit, take a Vapur from Karakoy to Kadikoy to see it."
– Turgut Akaçık, Autonomy

3 Perili Köşk
Map N, P.110

A gallery space for innovative exhibitions on weekends and an office during the week, the red brick mansion has a storied past. Ottoman statesman Yusuf Ziya Paşa commissioned the mansion for his family in the 1910s shortly before the outbreak of WWI and his bankruptcy. Locals' claim to see a ghostly silhouette in the largely unfinished property, earning it the nickname, *Perili Köşk*, Turkish for "haunted mansion". Featuring bricks imported from France, the house was restored and completed in 2000 by its current owner, Borusan Holdings, in harmony with its original plans.

🏠 *Rumeli Hisarı, Baltalimanı Hisar Cad. 5, Sarıyer*
🖉 *Borusan Contemporary: 1000-2000 (Sa-Su),*
except Jan 1 & the first days of religious holidays,
10 TL, www.borusancontemporary.com

*"Definitely visit the terrace to gaze at the Bosphorus!
This is one example of Istanbul's architectural
heritage near the magnificent Rumelian Castle."*

– Can Büyükberber

4 Galata Kulesi
Map A, P.104

Erected in the sixth century and rebuilt in 1348 as part of the city wall of the former Genoese colony, the Romanesque stone tower has survived fires and storms, served as an observatory tower, housed a dungeon and witnessed suicides. Its top is also rumoured to have been the point where the legendary Ottoman aviator Hezârfen Ahmed Çelebi took flight with his handmade wings. Standing at just about 68 metres on a steep hillside, the tower sticks out from its historic environs and offers a spectacular 360-degree view across the Golden Horn and the Bosphorus.

🕐 *0900–1900 daily* 💲 *20 TL*
🏠 *Bereketzade, Büyükhendek Sok., Beyoğlu*
🔗 *www.galatakulesi.org*

"Have a look at it at night when the tower seems magical with birds flying around it. The neighbourhood is also architecturally and culturally interesting."
– Ayşegül Akçay Kavakoğlu, İstanbul Kemerburgaz University

5 Balat
Map H, P.108

Bound by Fener and the Golden Horn, Balat was once a dynamic neighbourhood where Christians lived peacefully next to Muslims and Jews fleeing from Spain. The district began to fall into disrepair in the mid-1990s when the wealthier left for city life, but is slowly regaining its charm with UNESCO's support and artists start to claim the place. Be careful not to get lost in the labyrinth of cobbled streets flanked by colourful houses (*Merdivenli Yokuşu Sok.*) and traditional coffee shops. Try local meze at Cibalikapı Balıkçısı. Chora Church (*Kariye Kilisesi*), the Greek Orthodox Church of Aya Nikola and Rose Mosque (*Gül Camii*) all bear witness to the area's centuries of changes.

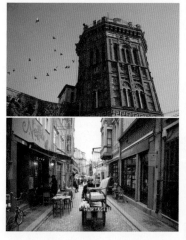

🏠 Balat, Fatih
🖉 Cibalikapı Balıkçısı Haliç: cibalikapibalikcisi.com

"*Visit the oldest surviving Fener Greek Orthodox College (Özel Fener Rum Lisesi) at Sancaktar Yks. 36, also known as the Red School, established in 1454.*"

– Murat Beşer

6 Galata Köprüsü
Map E, P.106

Spanning across the Golden Horn, the 490-metre bascule bridge presents a symbolic link between the old and the new. Sultanahmet on the west end had been the capitals of the Byzantine and Ottoman empires and therefore home to imperial palaces, principal mosques and ruined towns. Contrastingly, Karaköy on the other end oozes a wide range of urban vibes. The current Galata Bridge is the fifth to have stood on the site. One of the first bridge designs was proposed by Leonardo Da Vinci in 1502 but was never realised on this site. The design was later used as part of the Da Vinci Project and actualised in Ås, Norway in 2001.

🏠 *Sultanahmet, Fatih–Karaköy, Beyoğlu*

"The bridge is most lively in the early hours and has the most beautiful sunrise view in the city. Wake up early for a walk. Bring your camera and be ready for surprises!"

– Halit Fatih Kızılgök

022

7 Maçka Demokrasi Parkı
Map F, P.107

Greenery and parks are a rarity in an urbanised city like Istanbul. That's why Maçka Park is a heavenly respite from the city's humdrum, with its central location and its unique 15.6-hectare span of lawn and old trees punctuated by walking paths, fountains and ponds. Go for a warm summer picnic in a hidden corner with a lovely view over the Dolmabahçe Palace or take in its seasonal beauty with a leisurely stroll. Then end the visit with a short ride on a *teleferik* (cable car). The Taşkışla terminal is within a 15-minute walk from the bustling Taksim Square.

🏠 *Harbiye, Şişli*

"*Go on a lovely Sunday to feel the love in the air. Mingle with expats, acrobats, joggers and young parents scattering around the park like a fantastic board game.*"

– Volkan Dede, Walky-Talky

8 Ayasofya
Map G, P.108

Originating as a basilica ordered by Byzantine Emperor Justinian in the sixth century, Hagia Sophia, meaning "divine wisdom" in Greek, amazes visitors with its phenomenal mosaic art and its sheer size, especially its central dome. Its unusual scale required special materials from Greece, Egypt and Syria, and more than 10,000 architects and workers to complete the job. Following the conquest of Istanbul by Fatih Sultan Mehmed, the church was converted into a mosque in 1453 and a museum in 1935. The minarets were added after the conversion for announcements and calls to prayer.

🕐 Tu–Su: 0900–1900 (Apr 15–Oct 25), –1700 (Oct 26–Apr 14), opens in the afternoon on the first days of religious holidays 💲 30 TL
🏠 Sultanahmet, Ayasofya Meydanı, Fatih
📞 +90 212 522 1750, +90 212 522 0989
🔗 ayasofyamuzesi.gov.tr
✐ Last entry: one hour before closing

"It has an important place in the art world with its architecture, grandness, size and roles. Go to Sultanahmet, buy a simit and see the museum."
– Meltem Özbek

9 Yerebatan Sarayı
Map G, P.108

Descend some 50 stairs and enter this dank "Sunken Palace" built 1500 years ago by order of Byzantine Emperor Justinian I. As the largest surviving underground reservoir in the city, the Basilica Cistern has roughly 9,800 square metres of floor space and 80,000 cubic metres of water storage capacity. Replacing rowboat tours, elevated walkways now invite visitors to marvel at the chamber's depth under a vaulted ceiling held by 336 pillars, with unmatched bases believed to be scavenged from nearby Roman ruins. The Medusa heads at the northwest edge are most famous for their intriguing positions.

🕐 Daily: 0900–1830 (summer), –1730 (winter), opens at 1pm on Jan 1 & the first days of religious holidays 💲 20 TL 🏠 Sultanahmet, Alemdar Mah. 1/3, Yerebatan Cad., Fatih 📞 +90 212 512 1570 🔲 yerebatan.com

"Don't leave the city before you pay a good visit."

– Aykut Aydoğdu

10 Süleymaniye Camii
Map E, P.106

Perching atop one of Istanbul's seven hills, Sü-leymaniye's state-of-the-art design matches the glory of Süleyman the Magnificent, the Ottoman sultan who tasked architect Mimar Sinan with the job in 1550. At the age of 60, Sinan tackled the problematic site with superb spatial planning, topping off the multi-domed mosque with a stately interior, grand courtyards and charitable facilities. The four minarets with a total of ten balconies symbolise Süleyman as the tenth sultan of the Ottoman Empire. The sultan, his wife and the architect himself were all entombed within the compound and remain there to this day.

🕐 0900–1730 daily except prayer times
🏠 Beyazıt, Süleymaniye Mah., Fatih

"Sinan has more than 400 works in Istanbul, so try to see many while you are here. My favourites are Rüstem Paşa Mosque in Tahtakale and Selimiye Mosque in Edirne."

— Aslı Filinta

027

11 Kanyon
Map S, P.111

Istanbul is not all minarets and bazaars. A short ride on Istanbul's metro from Taksim will take you to Levent, one of the city's major financial districts where skyscrapers and new developments like Kanyon overshadow you. Introduced in 2006, Kanyon is an ensemble of modern offices, luxury residences and a shopping mall. Within the signature curving façade, white collar workers and shoppers unwind in its courtyards and semi-open air walkways that flow like a natural canyon. Keep your coat on if you're visiting on a cold day, as wind chills the place as much as the sun warms it up.

🕙 *1000-2200 daily*
🏠 *Levent, Büyükdere Cad. 185, Beşiktaş*
📞 *+90 212 353 5300*
URL *www.kanyon.com.tr*

"This is the best place to enjoy a late night movie, and a midday coffee between meetings."

– Tamer Nakışçı, Futureisblank

12 Caddebostan Konak

Map O, P.110

One of the many prominent architectural treasures the Ottomans had left all over the city is the lavishly designed mansions – "konak" in Turkish. A stroll along Caddebostan coast will lead you to Ragip Sarica Pasha Mansion built by August Jasmund, the architect behind İstanbul Sirkeci Terminal. Many more well-preserved examples can be found in Yıldız Park and Emirgan Park. Mansions on the waterfront, mainly along the shores of Bebek, Arnavutköy, Kanlıca, Kandilli and Yeniköy, are known as Yalı. The best way to get a sense of them is to take a special boat tour with Saffet Emre Tongu, a popular guide with deep knowledge of these properties.

🏠 Caddebostan, Kadıköy
🔗 Saffet Emre Tonguç: tonguc.info

"The Caddebostan mansion is a key meeting point of the Asian seaside. Have picnic or a stroll in the park, then hit the bars in Bağdat Street as the night falls."

– Volkan Yıldırmaz

Cultural & Art Spaces

Young galleries, innovative programmes and urban culture

Royal palaces, towering mosques and an exotic cuisine may have defined Istanbul in the past, but the contemporary art scene has been steadily growing since the 1980s, with new galleries popping up in Karaköy, Nişantaşı, Cihangir and other art-conscious neighbourhoods every few minutes over the the past decade.

Art enthusiasts must visit SALT (#17), especially the Galata branch for its awe-inspiring building. Arter (#14) and Istanbul'74 (#19) throw in a good mix of local and international artists' works. Street art, murals, and young artists' ateliers line the streets of Yeldeğirmeni (#21) on the Asian Side while the works of up-and-coming Turkish artists can be viewed at Öktem&Aykut (#15) on the European Side. For trippers planning a really short stay in Istanbul, maximise your time by visiting the beautiful Art Nouveau–style Misir Apartment (*Tomtom Mah., İstiklal Cad. 163, Beyoğlu*) houses top galleries, such as Galeri Nev, Nesrin Esirtgen Collection and Pi Artworks, and a clubby rooftop bar, 360.

The city's first modern museum Istanbul Modern (#13) has a great permanent collection as well as temporary exhibitions and it's a 5-minute walk from Karaköy, Istanbul's hippest neighbourhood full of creative minds. Visit Pera Museum (#16) and Sakıp Sabancı Museum (#22) for one-of-a-kind exhibitions.

Check IKSV's website (*www.iksv.org/en*) in advance of your trip to see if any of the festivals (theatre, jazz, film, music) or the Biennials will be on while you're in town.

Çelenk Bafra
Curator, Istanbul Modern

I worked at IKSV as the director of the Istanbul Biennial and advisor for the Pavilion of Turkey in the Venice Biennale. I now oversee the curatorial department at Istanbul Modern.

Arter
P.036

Hemi Behmoaras
Filmmaker

A Master's student in film making at Kadir Has University, I also work in music promoting gigs, book DJs for clubs and blend disco/house music as Pineapple Pop and as half of Paradisko.

Sinan Logie
Architect

I'm also an artist and urban activist with a background in skateboarding and street culture. I teach at Istanbul Bilgi University and co-write the book Istanbul 2023.

İstanbul
Modern
P.034

Öktem&Aykut
P.038

Dilara Karolina Sakpınar
Musician & singer-songwriter

I'm half Swedish and half Turkish. I enjoy experimenting various music genres. Apart from my band 123, I also go solo as Lara Di Lara and collaborate as Alike Places.

SALT
P.040

Sarp Sözdinler
Graphic designer

I founded my namesake studio in 2014 after working at practices such as Base Design, Bülent Erkmen's BEK and Daniska. I'm interested in editorial design and typography.

Selim Ünlüsoy
Ogilvy & Mather Istanbul

I'm the executive creative director at Ogilvy & Mather Istanbul. I paint things matte black in my spare time and publish works under the name Vögler + Schultz. Just because.

Pera Müzesi
P.039

santral-
istanbul
P.042

Esra Çoruh
Fashion writer

Starting out as an art director at Cosmopolitan, I've been writing about fashion for 20 years for newspapers Sabah and Habertürk. My website imfashion also talks about travel and food.

Depo
P.045

Elif Refiğ
Film director, Muhtelif Yapımlar

A MFA graduate in film at Columbia University, New York, I work project-based for film and TV companies. I love spending quality time with animals, friends, plants, films, music and books.

Merve Atılgan
Illustrator

I'm also a ballet dancer. I've been dancing since five and drawing since six. I mainly work on children's books, comics, concept art and character design. I love both of my professions.

Istanbul'74
P.044

Yeldeğirmeni
P.046

Tanla Özuzun
Documentary & event photographer

I adore horses. I manage a photography blog, an equestrian web portal and compete in showjumping events. I have a horse named Monti and a dog called Yufka.

Çıplak Ayaklar
Kumpanyası
P.048

Alican Tezer
Musician

I play for the bands Ayyuka, Insanlar and Buyuk Ev Ablukada and have worked as an art director for some time. I'm a big fan of rakı and love listening to music while walking on the street.

Melis Danişmend
Journalist & musician

Melis Danişmend has worked at Radikal, Sabah, Rolling Stone and InStyle. In her music career she has made two solo albums and gave concerts all around Turkey.

Sakıp
Sabancı
Müzesi
P.047

Souq
P.049

$$P_1 + \frac{1}{2}\rho v_1^2 + \rho g h_1 = P_2 + \frac{1}{2}\rho v_2^2 + \rho g h_2$$

13 İstanbul Modern

Map A, P.105

Since 2004, opening as the city's first privately-owned modern art museum, Istanbul Modern has been a game changer in the city's art scene. Its strong vision and global awareness regularly fill the 8,000-square-metre former warehouse with all things contemporary, from its own collection of 20th-century Turkish paintings to photography and video art created by the likes of Yoko Ono, Kutluğ Ataman and Mehmet Güleryüz. Keep your eye open for art as you might be walking on one, like Monica Bonvicini's Stairway to Hell (2003). Their music events, talks and alternative film screenings are also a big draw for cultural buffs.

🕐 1000–1800 (Tu–W, F–Su), –2000 (Th), except Jan 1 & the first day of religious holidays 💲 25/14 TL
🏠 Karaköy, Meclis-i Mebusan Cad., Liman İşletmeleri Sahası, Antrepo 4, Beyoğlu
📞 +90 212 334 7300 🌐 www.istanbulmodern.org
🖇 Guided tour: 10 TL (excl. entry), 4–20 pax., By appointment only.

"Don't miss the restaurant with a great view to the Bosphorus and historical peninsula, and the shop with all kinds of books and objects made by local designers."
– Çelenk Bafra, Istanbul Modern

14 Arter
Map A, P.104

Boasting an enormous display window, Arter is hard to miss on the busy İstiklal Street. Backed by Vehbi Koç Foundation, this gallery identifies itself simply as a "space for art". Experimental spirit keeps flowing through its historical four-storey showcase, connecting contemporary art to a broad audience. Whilst past shows have displayed international artists, its focus is on the Turkish art scene, introducing video and site-specific installations by the likes of Kutluğ Ataman, Ömer Ali Kazma and Füsun Onur. Despite being a young gallery, Arter has hosted exhibitions of the last two Istanbul Biennials, affirming its much revered reputation.

🕐 1100–1900 (Tu–Th), 1200–2000 (F–Su), except Jan 1 & the first days of Eid 🏠 Karaköy, İstiklal Cad. 211, Beyoğlu 📞 +90 212 708 5800
🔗 www.arter.org.tr

"If you wish to see proper Turkish modern art, this is the place. They have really bold exhibitions, each with a unique window display like a classy magazine cover."
– Hemi Behmoaras

15 **Öktem&Aykut**
Map A, P.105

Set up by Doga Oktem and Tankut Ayku, Öktem&Aykut's mission is to bring contemporary art, especially up-and-coming local artists to the forefront. The brand new addition to Istanbul's art scene provides a platform for young Turkish artists to be discovered and creates a bond between different generations of local artists. Situated in a central Galata location, tourists and locals alike can enjoy the gallery whilst in the neighbourhood.

🙂 *1200-1900 (Tu-Sa)*
🏠 *Karaköy, Büyük Hendek Cad., Portakal Sok. 2, Beyoğlu*
URL *oktemaykut.com*

"Art lovers should also have a look at Mısır Apartment for some of the city's major art galleries."
– Sinan Logie

16 Pera Müzesi
Map A, P.104

Catch a glimpse of the Ottomans' glory at Pera Museum through Suna and İnan Kıraç's goodly collection of Orientalist paintings and historical artefacts. The most famous piece of all is Osman Hamdi Bey's *The Tortoise Trainer* (1906) which captured the era's life in spectacular details. Pera's mission to preserve the Ottoman chapter of Turkish history is complete with the 19th-century building, formerly Hotel Bristol. Pera's big-name travelling exhibitions featuring the likes of Rembrandt, Frida Kahlo and Henri Cartier-Bresson are unmissable.

🕐 1000-1900 (Tu-Th, Sa), -2200 (F), 1200-1800 (Su), except Jan 1 & the first day of religious holidays
💲 20 TL/free admission after 1800 (F)
🏠 Tepebaşı, Meşrutiyet Cad. 65, Beyoğlu
📞 +90 212 334 9900 🔗 www.peramuzesi.org.tr

"The exhibitions here are very good but what I also like about Pera is the wonderful kids' section where children can come and make art."
– Dilara Karolina Sakpınar

17 SALT
Map A, P.104 & Map D, P.106

Take time to contemplate art at SALT. Funded by Garanti Bank and directed by veteran curator Vasif Kortun, the research centre explores critical issues in Turkey's contemporary visual and material culture, and invites dialogue between visitors and their spaces, across two venues. Both sites house a well-curated bookstore and run an integrated programme of exhibitions, film screenings and workshops, but SALT Galata also contains an open archive, a restaurant and a museum, with the Ottoman Bank building's past secured in its gigantic basement vaults.

🕐 1200–2000 (Tu–Sa), –1800 (Su), except Jan 1 & the first two days of Eid and Greater Eid
🏠🕐 Beyoğlu: Asmalımescit, İstiklal Cad. 136, Beyoğlu, +90 212 377 4200, Galata: Karaköy, Bankalar Cad. 11, Beyoğlu, +90 212 334 2200
🔗 saltonline.org 🖉 SALT Beyoğlu will temporarily suspend operations until further notice.

"SALT Galata is where you can enjoy being on your own and listen to your thoughts."
– Sarp Sözdinler, Studio Sarp Sözdinler

18 santralistanbul
Map L, P.110

By the Golden Horn on the grounds of Bilgi University, stands santralistanbul, formerly the Ottoman Empire's first urban-scale power plant. A thorough renovation in 1983 of the city's electricity supply facilitated the emergence of this source of art, culture and inspiration, impressive not only for what it contains but also for its remarkable architecture. The plant's original turbine rooms now comprise the Museum of Energy, while the maintenance and storage rooms have been converted into restaurants and entertainment venues. For your fix of reading materials, explore the Latif Mutlu Library, where prestigious journals, newspapers from nearly 100 countries, and thousands of e-books and e-magazines are kept.

🕘 0900-1800 daily except P.H.

🏠 Emniyettepe, Kazım Karabekir Cad. 2, Eyüp

URL www.santralistanbul.org

🖉 Free shuttle buses run daily from Kabataş Gangboard except P.H.. Energy Museum: 0900-1800 daily except P.H., Guided tour (TR/EN): 25/15 TL, max 25 pax.

"This is where I graduated from, which houses one of the coolest museums in the city. Be sure to stop by Otto, a restaurant and bar, for a shot or two if it's still there."

– Selim Ünlüsoy, Ogilvy & Mather Istanbul

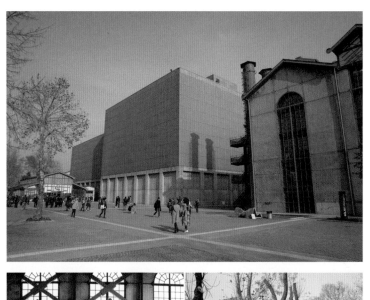

19 Istanbul'74
Map D, P.106

Istanbul'74 knows how to maintain an edge. More than just a gallery, 74 stages a unique mix of contemporary art with a multidisciplinary focus reflecting the founders' deep knowledge of fashion, photography and films, and a taste for classics. Apart from exhibitions, screenings and live performances spotlighting talents and legends, Istanbul'74 also organises the star-studded three-day public annual event, Istanbul International Arts and Culture Festival, and publishes bilingual periodicals on arts and culture under the name '74GAZETTE.

🕐 1100–1830 (M–F), 1300– (Sa) 🏠🕐 Galatasaray: Kuloğlu, Turnacıbaşı Cad. 9 Kat 2, Neşe Apt., Beyoğlu, +90 212 243 3948, Karaköy: Karaköy, Kemankeş Cad., Galata Sarap İskelesi Sok. 8/3, Beyoğlu, +90 212 244 2994 🔲 istanbul74.com

"*Visit both galleries to see the modern face of Istanbul.*"

– Esra Çoruh

20 Depo
Map A, P.104

Founded by cultural institution Anadolu Kültür, Depo is the first civic-minded project space in Istanbul that works to bring about regional cultural exchanges between Turkey, the Caucasus, the Middle East and the Balkans. Inside a defunct tobacco warehouse, exhibitions, screenings, conferences, talks and workshops take turns engaging an intellectual crowd made of artists, cultural operators, academicians and a curious public. Relevant research findings and recent cultural happenings in the region can be reviewed in Depo's multilingual quarterly e-journal *Red Thread*.

🕐 1100-1900 (Tu-Su) 🏠 Tophane, Tütün Deposu, Lüleci Hendek Cad. 12, Beyoğlu 📞 +90 212 292 3956
URL www.depoistanbul.net

"*Spare time to explore local neighbourhood practices in Tophane. Nice antique stores and the famous Museum of Innocence are just around the corner too.*"

– Elif Refiğ, Muhtelif Yapımlar

21 Yeldeğirmeni
Map K, P.109

With a synagogue, churches, and mosques within a stone's throw from each other, the amalgamation of different cultures has created a fundamental ground for inspiration in the bohemian Kadıköy neighbourhood. Recent regeneration projects have seen the historic Notre Dame du Rosaire Church become a cultural centre and a network of artists establishing small ateliers throughout the area like Arthereistanbul. Keep an eye out for murals covering many vacant walls, slowly becoming the canvases of international artists such as JAZ from Spain and Claudio Ethos from Brazil.

🏠 Yeldeğirmeni, Kadıköy
🔗 Yeldeğirmeni Sanat: kultursanat.
kadikoy.bel.tr/tr/kultur-merkezleri/
yeldegirmeni-sanat

"Yeldeğirmeni is like an open-air art gallery. Definitely worth a visit to see the street art done by many artists from various parts of the world."

– Merve Atılgan

22 Sakıp Sabancı Müzesi

Map M, P.110

Built in 1925, Sakıp Sabancı Museum's main
building used to be known as Atlı Köşk (Horse
Mansion) because of the two horse sculptures
installed in the garden. Partially preserved in
their original settings, a substantial collection
of calligraphy art, painting, decorative arts and
furniture acquired by its last occupants, the
late business tycoon and philanthropist Sakıp
Sabancı and his father, welcomes visitors in
the house. Its annexed gallery blends works of
contemporary and modern artists like Anish
Kapoor, Abidin Dino and Auguste Rodin. Stop by
the gift shop on your way out for unique mer-
chandise inspired by the museum's collection.

🕐 1000–1800 (Tu, Th–Su), –2000 (W)
💲 20/10 TL/free admission (W) 🏠 Emirgan,
Sakıp Sabancı Cad. 42, Sarıyer 📞 +90 212 277 2200
🌐 www.sakipsabancimuzesi.org

"Its restaurant, Müzedechanga, is impressive by
style, as well as the food and view it offers. Saturday
and Sunday brunches are recommended."

– Tanla Özuzun

23 Çıplak Ayaklar Kumpanyası
Map A, P.104

Born from a liberal vision for innovative art, Çıplak Ayaklar Kumpanyası experiments with dance, theater, music, and video art. Against all forms of violence and discrimination and in search of a land of dreams, the close-knit group that makes up Çıplak Ayaklar Kumpanyası has spent the past 15 years organising festivals, collaborating with international choreographers, showcasing exhibitions, putting up concerts and multidisciplinary shows, and much more. If you want an out-of-the-box performance, this is the venue to check out.

🕐 Showtime varies with programmes
🏠 Firuzağa, Çukurcuma Cad. 6/3, Beyoğlu
📞 +90 539 459 9534
f Ciplak Ayaklar Kumpanyasi
URL www.ciplakayaklar.com

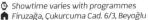

"This is where Istanbul's best and most creative artists and musicians gather together to create and perform. Check out their website for upcoming events."

– Alican Tezer

24 Souq

Map A, P.104

What was once the city's best curated pop-up bazaar founded by Yaprak Aras, former features editor at Vogue Turkey, finally established a permanent home in Karaköy. The pull of Souq is its meticulous collection of artisanal, vintage, handmade, designer goodies, good music and great coffee perfectly merged together under one roof, drawing local creators, artists and entrepreneurs to come to rub shoulders or even seek out collaboration opportunities. Check for their monthly theme on their facebook page and don't forget to rummage in their 1970s psychedelic record collection.

Opening hours vary with events
Karaköy, Murakıp Sok. 12A, Beyoğlu
Souq Karaköy

"It has a welcoming atmosphere where you can find anything from vintage items to Turkish designer's pieces. Go early to get your hands on the nicer items."

– Melis Danişmend

Markets & Shops

Food shopping, concept stores and antique finds

Gone are the days when shopping in Istanbul was limited to the bazaars, although they still offer great finds. With the creative world on the rise, Istanbul's shopping scene dances between the traditional and the contemporary with perfect poise.

Spend a day exploring Çukurcuma (#34), going in and out of vintage stores and antique shops, with coffee breaks at the recently-opened cafés like Cuma (*Çukurcuma Cad. 51*) and Holy Coffee (*Kuloglu, Hacioglu Sok. 1B*). If you want to take your hunt to another level, Dolapdere Sunday Market (#35) offers an entirely different experience full of treasures scavenged from all sorts of places.

Concept stores are popping everywhere, with many lining up around Serdar-ı Ekrem Street in Galata (#29). Pay a visit to FEY (#28) for great style finds, Mae Zae (#30) for books, handmade goods, and vintage pieces all under the same roof, and Shopi go No:17 (#2) for a selection of international designer pieces from bicycles to magazines.

Gifts are to be bought while at the Grand Bazaar, no doubt. Be targeted in your approach to avoid being flogged random items. Abdulla (#31), Şişko Osman (*Kapalıçarşı Zincirli Han 15*), and Sivaslı Istanbul Yazmacısı (*Yağlıkcılar Sok. 57*) should be on your bucket list for quality towels, hand-printed fabrics and Turkish rugs. Food shopping is best done at specialty stores. Head to Baylan (#32) for desserts, the century-old Meşhur Bebek Badem Ezmesi (*Bebek, Cevdet Paşa Cad. 53/C, Beşiktaş*) for the best *marzipans*, NAR Gourmet at Istinye Park Mall for jams and olive oil (*Istinye Bayırı Cad. 73, Sarıyer*), and Selamlique at Kanyon (#11) for luxurious Turkish coffee blends.

Duygu Altıparmak
Fashion editor

I've been working with magazines, brands and agencies as a fashion consultant since 2005. I now work actively on men's fashion with Esquire, GQ, Elele and Cosmopolitan.

Shopi go
No:17
P.056

Emre Özücoşkun
Co-founder, cisimdesign

I'm an interior architect, having designed a wide range of interior spaces from residences to offices since 2010. In recent years I focus on restaurant and café design.

Yasemin Arpaç
Interior architect, Ofist

I run design company Ofist in the bohemian district of Beyoğlu with my partner. I am quite an hyperactive person. I like to feel the city by walking or travelling.

Sanayi 313
P.054

ECNP Gallery
P.057

Galata
P.059

Gül Ağış
Fashion designer, LUG VON SIGA

Upon graduation with a Master's degree in fashion design from University Politecnico di Milano, I started at Costume National and created her own label LUG VON SIGA in Istanbul in 2010.

Nilay Özlü
Architect

I am a curious soul, a traveller, a historian, an art-lover, a dedicated reader and not-so-dedicated writer. A PhD student, a teacher, a mother and an activist.

Hande Oynar
Editor-in-Chief, Luxos

I'm a fashion and luxury editor by day, arts and travel writer by night, and a contemporary art tour guide in between. A mother of two dragons and a long-haired dachshund.

FEY
P.058

Mae Zae
P.060

Zeynep Erdoğan
Fashion designer

My customised designs first appeared in Milan's concept stores. I set up my own showroom at my home city Istanbul in 2008 and continued the creation of street-couture.

Baylan Pastanesi
P.062

Eylül Aslan
Photographer

I was born in Istanbul in 1990 and studied French Literature at the Istanbul University. My debut photography book *Trauerweide* was published in 2013, followed by *DEAR SLUT* in 2015.

Ahmet Uluğ
Founding partner, Pozitif

I've been fostering Istanbul's major concert and music festivals with Pozitif since 1989. Pozitif also manages performance venues Babylon, Blackbox Istanbul and record label Doublemoon.

Abdulla
@Kapalı Çarşı
P.061

Kadıköy Tarihi Balıkçılar Çarşısı
P.063

Muhsin Akgün
Photographer

I started professional photography in 1995. I mostly take portraits and capture performances. I have worked for media and art institutions like İKSV, Pozitif and Doğan Medya Grubu.

Dolapdere Bit Pazarı
P.066

Mari Spirito
Director, Protocinema

I open up opportunities for emerging artists and curators with Protocinema and provide mentorship at PROTO5533. I was an advisor for the Mardin Biennial and Art Basel programmes.

Aylin Güngör
Publisher & photographer

I've been running Bant Magazine, a monthly on music, cinema and art, together with James Hakan Dedeoğlu since 2004. I currently reside in Moda.

Çukurcuma
P.064

Tahtakale
P.067

25 Sanayi 313
Map Q, P.111

A base for good food, design, and inspiration, Sanayi 313 is located in an old car repair shop, in the industrial Maslak neighbourhood. Interior designer and a naturally-curious aesthetics-hunter Enis Karavil, along with his brother Amir, a businessman, established Sanayi 313, creating a novelty amongst the industrial surroundings of Maslak. Sanayi 313 features a curated collection of fashion, furnishings, and food, mainly international imports ranging from pens and bow ties to soaps and candles. You'll also find Serena Uziyel's modern, handmade shoes and bags featuring traditional craftsmanship are sold here as well.

🕐 0800–1800 (M–F), 1000– (Sa)
🏠 Maslak, Atatürk Oto Sanayi Sitesi 2, Kısım 10, Sok. 313, Sarıyer
📞 +90 212 286 3857
URL www.sanayi313.com

"It has a healthy and organic restaurant. Try their baked pumpkin, limy meatball and strawberry pie!"
– Duygu Altıparmak

26 Shopi go No:17
Map F, P.107

What started out as an online concept store evolved into a physical store in one of Nişantaşı's trendiest streets. Shopi go is dedicated to creating a space filled with style, quality, and design at its best, serving as an urban heaven to the cool creative crowd with a taste for enviable goods. The store brings together the latest collections of over 250 designers, including names like Rachel Zoe, American Retro, Wood Wood and Tokyobike. Clothes, personal care products, books, magazines, toys, home décor items, shoes, bags and accessories are all up for sale here.

🕙 1000-1930 (M-Sa), 1100-1800 (Su)
🏠 Nişantaşı, Mim Kemal Öke Cad. 17/1, Şişli
📞 +90 212 296 9661
URL shopigo.com

"Take time to browse through their fantastic reference book collection!"

– Emre Özücoşkun, cisimdesign

27 ECNP Gallery
Map F, P.107

'Less is more' is the philosophy behind the fine contemporary jewellery and homewares at ECNP, a store and gallery initiated by designers Ela Cindoruk and Nazan Pak. Using innovative methods and materials, such as paper, epoxy resin, titanium and niobium, as well as traditional materials like pearls, gold and silver, each of Cindoruk and Pak's creations reflect a commitment to their design aesthetic. Check out their in-house gallery to view works by other designers.

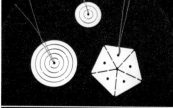

🕓 1400–1900 (M), 1100– (Tu–Sa)
🏠 Teşvikiye, Ahmet Fetgari Sok. 56-A, Şişli
☎ +90 212 219 6292
🔗 ecnp-jewelry.com

"Ela and Nazan pioneer contemporary jewellery design in Turkey. Snatch some newspaper coasters if other designs exceed your budget."

– Yasemin Arpaç, Ofist

28 FEY
Map F, P.107

A museum-like boutique with clothes and accessories displayed like works of art, FEY is a breath of fresh air in the uber-fashionable Nişantaşı neighbourhood with its grounded elegance and deep-seated sophistication. The boutique is owned by Marie Claire Turkey's long-time general manager and publishing director Fatoş Yalın, a style icon who embodies grace and confidence. Her own creations of timeless men's and women's collections are sold alongside pieces by Turkish designers, exceptional vintage pieces, miscellaneous books and decorative items. Expect to find classy, minimalist, and simply chic items here.

🕐 1000–1900 (M-Sa)
🏠 Nişantaşı, Mim Kemal Öke Cad. 9, Şişli
📞 +90 212 219 8724 **URL** www.fey.com.tr

"Relax you as soon as you cross its threshold and lose yourself in its vintage accessory collection."

– Gül Ağış, LUG VON SIGA

29 Galata
Map A, P.104

One of the oldest neighbourhoods of Istanbul, Galata now draws crowds with its beautiful architecture, cosy cafés and the Galata Tower (#4), its main attraction. Start walking down Galip Dede Street at the very end of Istiklal Street marked by Mawlawi House Museum and Tünel, the world's third-oldest subway. Flanking the street are shops that sell handmade musical instruments, juice and some standard souvenir. For a real retail relief, turn left at a T-intersection after a long walk down the hill into the narrow Serdar-ı Ekrem Street, filled with concept stores and vintage shops. Décor lovers should turn right for Hiç Contemporary Crafts at Lüleci Hendek Sok. 35.

🏠 Galata, Galip Dede Cad., Çamekan Sok., Serdar-ı Ekrem Sok., Beyoğlu

"The best way to experience the area is by discovering small side streets and entering apartments and backyards."
– Nilay Özlü

30 Mae Zae

Map A, P.104

Owner and designer Münire Alabaz defines her
concept store as a life store, collecting objects
that inspire her. Part of the store is Alabaz's office and a corner is a café–cum–hangout space
with friends and visitors. The rest of the place
is dedicated to her findings, from custom-
made infinity mirrors to handmade pillows,
vintage items and books to pieces by local
designers including Studio B!st bags and Yuka
jewellery. A variety of workshops in collaboration with local creatives are held periodically
which she announces on Instagram.

🕐 1100–1900 daily 🏠 Karaköy, Kemankeş
Karamustafa Paşa Mah., Hoca Tahsin Sok. 16A,
Beyoğlu 📞 +90 212 288 7768 URL maezae.com

"If you go there in the winter, head for the fireplace
and ask for a hot chocolate with marshmallows while
you mingle with Alfie, the Golden Retriever."

– Hande Oynar, Luxos

31 Abdulla @Büyük Çarşı

Map G, P.108

Finding a gift may come as an unexpected challenge at the Grand Bazaar with vendors throwing themselves your way trying to lure you into their shops with one of the many languages they think they speak. Abdulla stands out from the chaos with its calm and collected store, offering all-natural Turkish classics like handmade olive-oil soaps, hand-loomed *peştemals* (linen towels), scrubbing mitts and brushes, linen sheets, decorative copper and metals bowls, and much more. The prices are higher than many of the other shops selling similar products but what you'll get here is totally splurge-worthy.

🕓 0900-1900 (M-Sa) 🏠 *Grand Bazaar: Mollafenari, Alibaba Türbe Sok. 25, Fatih*
📞 *+90 212 526 3070* URL *www.abdulla.com*

"*Don't waste time on the busy main streets of the Bazaar, get lost in the narrow ones.*"

– Zeynep Erdoğan

32 Baylan Pastanesi
Map I, P.109

As the only surviving branch of the famous patisserie founded by Filip Lenas who migrated from Albania to Istanbul in 1919, Baylan is worth a visit for its food alone. The original Beyoğlu branch was once a meeting point for writers and intellectuals in the 1950s. There is even a literary trend known as *Baylancılar Akımı*, referring to the social realist movement of those writers. Lenas' eldest son Harry learned the tricks of the trade at the Beyoğlu branch before it closed and takes Baylan further in the world of cakes and desserts. The Baylan classics, *Adisababa*, a slice of ice-cream cake, and *Kup Griye*, made with ice cream, caramel sauce, pistachio and almonds, are two of his best creations.

🕐 0700-2200 daily
🏠 Muvakkithane Cad. 9/A, Kadıköy
📞 +90 216 346 6350

"Try their specialty Kup Griye, but do not forget to try Adisababa either."

– Eylül Aslan

33 Kadıköy Tarihi Balıkçılar Çarşısı
Map I, P.109

Encapsulated within the larger Kadıköy Bazaar, Kadıköy's historic fish market is one of Istanbul's most popular places to shop. Concentrated mainly on one street, on the edge of Galata Bridge (#6), the fish market begins with traditional fishermen selling the freshest catches. As you walk up towards the heart of the market, the fishermen give way to down-to-earth fish restaurants where meze, a selection of hot and cold appetizers and rakı are enjoyed alongside what's in season.

🏠 Caferağa, Kadıköy Çarşısı, Kadıköy
🖉 Kadı Nimet Balıkçılık: 1130–0030 daily, Caferağa, Serasker Cad. Tarihi Balıkcılar Carsisi 10/A, Caferağa, +90 216 348 7389, www.kadinimet.com

"Eat fish at Kadı Nimet. Just choose your fish before entering the restaurant and have them cook it for you the way you want it."
– Ahmet Uluğ, Pozitif

34 Çukurcuma
Map A, P.104

Tucked away by the surrounding Cihangir and Galatasaray neighbourhoods, Çukurcuma's winding streets are Istanbul's answer to a time machine. Filled with antique stores, vintage shops, design boutiques and the newly-emerging restaurants and cafés, this relatively quiet area mesmerises with its architecture, channels the 1950s with a love letter or transports you back to the 1970s with an absurdly red coffee table. Nobel laureate Orhan Pamuk's Museum of Innocence, which exhibits the world he created in his 2008 novel of the same name, is well worth a visit.

🏠 Firuzağa, Beyoğlu
🔗 Museum of Innocence: 1000-1800 (Tu-W, F-Su), -2100 (Th), 25 TL, Firuzağa, Çukurcuma Cad., Dalgıç Çıkmazı 2, Beyoğlu, en.masumiyetmuzesi.org

"Get lost in the streets."
– Muhsin Akgün

35 Dolapdere Bit Pazarı
Map F, P.107

The Dolapdere Sunday Market is akin to a fantastical journey rather than an average day of shopping, bringing together all sorts of Istanbulites who are on the hunt for treasures amongst the hundreds of stands and stools. Owned by mainly the city's ethnic minorities, items up for grabs range from pens and clothes to old dentists' equipment, musical instruments, DVDs, magazines from the 80s, toys, and much more. The flea market has items mostly scavenged from trash so don't expect to find any antiques. Check out the Panagia Evangelistria Church while you're browsing.

🕐 *Early morning till late (Su)*
🏠 *Yenişehir, Dolapdere Cad., Beyoğlu*

"Go early. It is a rare authentic flea market with everything from trash to treasures for just a few Lira."

– Mari Spirito, Protocinema

36 Tahtakale
Map E, P.106

If you're prepared for the hassle and noise of jam-packed streets, crying and screaming children, and women dedicated to getting the best bargain from fed-up vendors, put on your best spirits and head to Tahtakale. Prepare to find shop after shop after shop selling absolutely anything and everything including 1,001 kinds of magnets, copper pots, firecrackers, tea sets, spices, toys, wigs, umbrellas of all shapes and sizes, crowns made of fake flowers and stores specialising in evil eye products. You can finesse the art of bargaining here if you haven't already done so at the Grand Bazaar (#31).

🏠 Tahtakale, Fatih

"Take your time and wander down this maze of wonders, weird shops and surprises."

– Aylin Güngör, Bant Magazine

Restaurants & Cafés

Glorious kebabs, ancient recipes and contemporary cuisine

Food forms the fiber of Istanbulites' beings, and all social gatherings revolve around it, accompanied by tea, coffee, *ayran* or *rakı* (aniseed-based national alcoholic drink). To experience Istanbul like a local, be prepared to eat a lot and very often.

Weekend breakfasts mean a couple of friends gather around a table and share all sorts of bread, jam, cheese, *menemen* (eggs done Turkish style with tomatoes and peppers), *bal-kaymak* (honey and clotted cream), and *gözleme* (flatbread filled with cheese and/or other fillings). Brunch with a view of the Bosphorus at the trendy Mangerie (*Cevdet Paşa Cad. 69, Bebek*) or the down-to-earth Sade (*Yahya Kemal Cad. 20/A, Rumelihisarı*). Or try great regional specialties from the east at Van Kahvaltı Evi (*Kılıç Ali Paşa Mah., Defterdar Yokuşu 52/A, Cihangir*) without the views.

Kebab is best left to dinner time, otherwise you might find it hard to walk around after a huge meal of starters, meat and desserts. Visit the Egyptian Bazaar late in the afternoon, and end the day on a high note at Hamdi (*Rüstem Paşa Mh., Tahmis Cad, Kalçın Sok. 11, Eminönü*), located just a few steps from the bazaar. If you'd be willing to trek around the city for great meat, look no further than Ali Haydar (*Gümüş Yüzük Sok. 6, Samatya*).

Modernised local favorites find themselves presented in a totally new light at Münferit (#43) and Gümrük (#39). Yet it would be a shame to leave the city before having a royal meal at Asitane (#47) where hundreds of years old Ottoman recipes are prepared with the utmost attention to detail as if serving to an actual sultan.

Emrah Özhan
Founder, DRAMATIC

I studied graphic design at Mimar Sinan University of Fine Arts. I started tattooing when I was 20 years old and started my own studio in 2013. I currently live and work at Moda, Istanbul.

Kafe Ara
P.074

Coşkun Aşar
Photographer

I use photography to tell stories. I like to live and work in dark and chaotic places.

Çiya Sofrası
P.072

Pemra Ataç Açıktan
Partner, Daniska & Rabarba

I'm the creative head of Daniska and Rabarba. I'm honoured to be selected as Eczacıbaşı Foundation's Young Graphic Designer of the Year twice and Ad Age's 2014 Women to Watch shortlist.

Gümrük
P.075

James Hakan Dedeoğlu
Publisher & musician

I run Bant Magazine with Aylin Güngör since 2004. We also organise concerts, exhibitions, screenings and panels. I also work as a writer, promoter and radio host.

Akali
P.078

Beril Ateş
Illustrator

I'm a wanderer inspired by new cities and cultures. My work is based on the concept of human minds which I also transform into design products under my brand, KAFA çizimhane.

Hazal Yılmaz
Blogger

I'm an urban blogger, a traveller, curious mind and serial writer living on a luggage in Istanbul. I walk 20K in a good day. I love waking up at dawn, a good Bloody Mary and Mexican food.

Yanyalı
Fehmi
Lokantası
P.076

Journey
P.079

Seyhan Özdemir Sarper
Co-founder, Autoban

I set up design studio Autoban with Sefer Çağlar. We work across architecture and interiors that constitute the cityscape of Istanbul and major cities around the world.

Çiçek Pasajı
P.081

Serdar Yılmaz
Art director

I make experimental films, video installations and art direct features and documentaries. My short movie Fried Chicken was shown at Cannes and Brooklyn Film Festivals in 2012.

Can Dağarslanı
Photographer & architect

I combine my architectural knowledge with photography in addition to a hidden interest for Jean-Luc Godard. My work is characterised by the expressive use of colours and natural light.

Münferit
P.080

Dandin
Bakery
P.082

Burcu Denizer
Owner, Kiki

I am a professional cook and crazy about breadmaking. I run the restaurant & bar Kiki. I love my neighbourhood, my city and my job. In the summer I go to southern Turkey for kiteboarding.

Asitane
Restaurant
P.084

Oktar Akın
Leo Burnett Istanbul

I'm a creative director. My job is not about advertising but people and observing their behaviour. In my spare time, I cook. I believe in culinary therapy, so I slice and dice!

Ertaç Uygun
Graphic designer

I'm also a DJ, record collector, podcaster and photographer. Music and design are the two things that I love in my life. I usually design for musicians and record labels, focusing on album covers.

Kantin
P.083

Mandabat-
maz
P.085

37 Çiya Sofrası
Map I, P.109

If you have just one day on Istanbul's Asian side and you're after a bite to eat, don't look any further than Çiya. A culinary legend and a true testament to the range of Turkish cuisine, Çiya is a family business with three branches right next to each other. The modest setting lets the widely acclaimed food do the talking with nearly 1,000 different dishes served each year, inspired by Southeastern Turkish, Syrian, Georgian and Iranian cuisine. You'll always find something original when you go. Owner Musa Dağdeviren, a foodie at heart has established a research institute and a culinary magazine on Turkish food and culture, sharing his knowledge and passion with the masses.

🕐 1100–2200 daily
🏠 Caferağa, Güneşli Bahçe Sok. 43, Kadıköy
📞 +90 216 330 3190
🌐 www.ciya.com.tr

"This is a great place to discover old and new traditional Anatolian cuisine."

– Emrah Özhan, DRAMATIC

38 Kafe Ara
Map D, P.106

If the waves of crowds on Istiklal Street make you feel uneasy, take refuge on a tiny side street right by the Galatasaray High School. Located below famous Turkish photographer Ara Güler's studio, Kafe Ara is a down-to-earth and calm establishment. If you see an old, bearded man sitting inside, it's most likely Ara Güler himself, who is a regular. Adorning the walls and placemats are his photos, giving the café a nostalgic atmosphere. The food is a variety of Turkish and Mediterranean fare and changes seasonally. The *Balkan Kofte* (Meatballs) is one of their specialities.

🕐 0730–0000 (M–Th), –0100 (F), 1030– (Sa), 1000–0000 (Su)
🏠 Tomtom, Tosbağa Sok. 2, Beyoğlu
📞 +90 212 245 4105 📖 kafeara.com

"Ask the manager if you can visit Güler's studio upstairs. He's most noted for photographing Istanbul in the 1950s, 60s, and 70s."

– Coşkun Aşar

39 Gümrük
Map A, P.104

Born from the Istanbulites responsible for the much loved Kafe Ara, Gümrük lives in a renovated historic building dating back to 1905. Industrial details, a nautical feel, and respected Ara Güler's photography art create a uniquely minimalist yet accessible space. Greek chef Stavriani Zervakakou's love affair with food offers her unique take on what could best be described as contemporary Turkish cuisine, changing the menu on a daily basis. Boutique Turkish wines, local and international beers, and coffee beans from around the globe make their way to Gümrük as well.

🕙 1000–0000 (M–Sa) 🏠 Karaköy, Kemankeş Karamustafa Paşa Mah., Gümrük Sok. 4, Beyoğlu
📞 +90 212 244 2252 URL karakoygumruk.com.tr

"Take time to explore the building floor by floor. There is a mini exhibition area dedicated to Ara Güler."

– Pemra Ataç Açıktan, Daniska & Rabarba

40 Yanyalı Fehmi Lokantası
Map I, P.109

Known for its delicious Turkish and Ottoman dishes made from high-quality ingredients, Yanyalı Fehmi is an ideal lunch spot where you can sample a variety of classic dishes. Conceived in late 19th century, the restaurant has a regal past as it was established by Fehmi Sönmezler, a Greece migrant to Constantinople, alongside his father Hüseyin Horp, who worked at the Ottoman palace, as his head chef. The restaurant maintains the same principle of quality and tradition as when it first opened. Highlights include *Yanya Köfte* (mince wrapped in aubergine) and *Hünkar Beğendi* (lamb stew served on creamy roasted eggplant puree), which literately translates as "Sultan delight".

🕐 1030–2230 daily
🏠 Osmanağa, Yağlıkçı İsmail Sok. 1, Kadikoy 📞 +90 216 336 3333
🔗 www.fehmilokantasi.com

"*Nothing fancy, very simple and very Turkish and also very delicious. Definitely try Hünkar Beğendi!*"

– James Hakan Dedeoğlu, Bant Magazine

41 Akali

Part artisanal bakery, part gastropub, and a full on design café, Akali cooks up a wide range of delicious and aesthetically pleasing dishes including homemade pasta, bread, egg-filled croissants, cheesecake, brownies and sandwiches. A pub and a bakery under the same roof may seem like an unlikely pairing but once the day's café vibe gives way to an after-work meet-up spot with a beer selection that includes Muğla's artisanal ale Gara Guzu, it makes perfect sense.

🕙 0800–2300 (Tu–F), 1000– (Sa), –1800 (Su)
📍 Maçka, Vişnezade Mah., Dibekçi Sok. 11A, Şişli
📞 +90 212 227 4242 📘 Akali

"Alkali team is just great! It's where you can make yourself at home. Any sandwich with special 'Kıstırma' bread is yummy!"

– Beril Ateş

42 Journey
Map A, P.104

A classic spot in the Cihangir neighbourhood filled with expats and bohemians, Journey is a laid-back restaurant with comfy sofas and a cosy vibe. Organic chicken, Himalayan salt, free-range eggs, and olive oil from Edremit are just some of the high-quality, bio-friendly, and health-conscious ingredients used in the kitchen. The pancakes, homemade granola and bountiful breakfast platters make it a popular spot for weekend brunches. Rye dough pizza fresh from the oven, green vegetables with quinoa and traditional Turkish dishes create a diverse offering, making it easy for anyone to find something they like on the menu.

🕐 0900–0200 daily 🏠 Cihangir, Akarsu Cad. 21A, Beyoğlu 📞 +90 212 244 8989
🔗 www.journeycihangir.com

"Journey has great vegetarian choices as well. Try the root vegetable salad. You'll love it!"

– Hazal Yılmaz

43 Münferit
Map A, P.104

True to its name, which translates to 'individual', Münferit is known for its unique flavour-bursting dishes, hip crowd, and post-dinner partying. A modern take on the classic Turkish tavern, the wood-panelled, dimly-lit, art-deco interior is quite a romantic setting for dinner. The contemporary Turkish menu features 21st-century versions of Turkish mezes, a selection of dips, salads, seafood and meat, all with extra flavour and foxiness. The rakı of choice here is Beylerbeyi rakı, named after an area of the city, and is arguably one of the best in the market.

🕐 1200–0230 daily
🏠 Firuzağa, Yeni Carsi Cad. 19, Beyoğlu
📞 +90 212 252 5067
URL munferit.com.tr

"Be sure to grab a table at the mews-like terrace and order the Turkish white cheese baked with porcini and truffle oil and the black couscous topped with calamari."
– Seyhan Özdemir Sarper, Autoban

44 Çiçek Pasajı
Map D, P.106

Loved by locals and visitors looking for a night of meze and rakı, Çiçek Pasajı is a classic Beyoğlu spot. Live musicians weave through the tables creating a vibrant and lively atmosphere. The restaurant complex is the namesake of the surrounding area, known as 'flower passage' where an arcade was built on the site where a theatre was destroyed during a fire in 1870. Some restaurants started putting their tables outside which led to the many eateries that now exist today. Although the arcade has lost its original feel, it's still worth a visit to one of the many eateries.

🕐 1100–0000 daily
🏠 Hüseyinağa, İstiklal Cad., Saitpaşa Geçidi 176/6, Beyoğlu URL www.tarihicicekpasaji.com

"Come here at night and have dinner at one of the fish restaurants. Make sure you ask for the price before ordering."

– Serdar Yılmaz

45 Dandin Bakery
Map A, P.104

Long before the Karaköy emerged as the cultural hub that it is today, designer couple Esra Dandin and Egemen Şenkardeş turned their workshop into a modern, charming bakery. The spacious high-ceilinged space is adorned with mint-green details and all of the furniture has been hand-made by the owners. A wide range of treats are on offer including banana and chocolate chip cookies, classic scones, shortbread, Madeleine cakes, and French pastries like religieuses. They also offer a daily lunch and dinner menu, which can be found on their website.

🕐 1000–2300 daily 🏠 Karaköy, Kemankeş Karamustafa Paşa Mah., Kılıç Ali Paşa Mescidi Sok. 17A, Beyoğlu 📞 +90 212 245 3369
📘 Dandin Bakery 🔗 www.dandin.co

"Try their lavender cake along with a herbal tea."
– Can Dağarslanı

46 Kantin

Map F, P.107

Kantin was born out of chef and owner Şemsa Denizel's vision of creating a humble *esnaf lokantası* (tradesmen restaurant) with an emphasis on fresh, seasonal ingredients and light dishes for the posh Nişantaşı crowd. Over the past 15 years, Kantin moved beyond that vision, becoming a simple and classy spot serving the self-dubbed 'new Istanbul cuisine'. White linen-clad tables, chalk boards and beautifully presented bakery goods create an elegant yet down-to-earth setting. Enjoy a sit-down lunch or stop by and try some of their home-made sundries like pesto, mayo and jams.

🕐 1100-1900 (M), 0830- (Tu-Sa)
🏠 Nişantaşı, Akkavak Sokağı 30, Şişli
📞 +90 212 219 3114
URL www.kantin.biz

"Avoid visiting at midday as it's usually packed."

– Burcu Denizer, Kiki

47 Asitane Restaurant
Map H, P.108

A testament to the culinary heritage that has led to sophisticated Turkish cuisine, Asitane is truly one of a kind, offering royal dishes from the Ottoman Palaces in its understated location right by the Chora Church. Although the recipes of dishes cooked for the Sultans were historically treated as secret, the Asitane team uncovered many of them after thorough research of official documents. The food here is expectedly superior as it was once fit for the Sultans. The flavours are quite different than what you'd find at most Turkish restaurants, offering a unique taste experience.

🕐 *1200–2300 daily*
🏠 *Edirnekapı, Kariye Camii Sok. 6, Fatih*
📞 *+90 212 635 7997*
🔗 *www.asitanerestaurant.com*

"*Asitane has a rotating menu that revives forgotten Ottoman recipes such as the Aphrodisiac food. Don't forget to chug some good old 'rakı'.*"

– Oktar Akın, Leo Burnett Istanbul

48 Mandabatmaz

Map D, P.106

With a plethora of places to get Turkish coffee, and hundreds of new trendy cafés opening up around the city, it can be a mission to find a good brew. Thankfully, Mandabatmaz is tried and trusted option, remaining as humble as it was since the day it opened in 1992, doing what it does best: serving Turkish coffee made the traditional way. If you're not used to strong black coffee, add some sugar so it packs less punch. And if you're not into coffee, try one of their fresh teas.

🕐 1000–2330 daily
🏠 Asmalımescit, İstiklal Cad., Olivia Geçidi 1A, Beyoğlu 🔗 www.mandabatmaz.com.tr

> *"If you want to take a break from the chaos of Istiklal Street and drink some quality Turkish coffee, this is the perfect spot."*
>
> – Ertaç Uygun

Nightlife

Live music, aniseed-flavoured nights and wild parties

Rivaling European party capitals with an undeniable cool factor, Istanbul's nightlife is uniquely diverse, offering up an eclectic mix of everything from the trendy and wild, to the sophisticated and intimate, in the shape of cocktail bars, jazz clubs, live-music venues, nightclubs, and taverns.

A fine line separates, or shall we say merges the dining scene and the buzzing nightlife scene, so start your night getting food to fuel a long night out at Çiçek Pasajı (#44) or Münferit (#43).

Non-party goers can find themselves fulfilled going home after a few drinks on the dinner table, but those who are out for a wild night will flock to Beyoğlu for a night of pub-crawling. Start out with a gig at Babylon (#58) or Salon İKSV (#59) surrounded by the city's creative crowd, and stop by a few legitimate bars at Barba (#51) or Muaf (#49) to make sure your blood-alcohol levels are up to speed.

Do what Istanbulites do best and head for a club with a fantastic view of the city. Let the Old City and the Galata Tower be your reference point as you dance at Karaköy's rooftop Zelda Zonk (#7) or get intimate with the glitterati at Anjelique (#56) with a Bosphorus view that mesmerises regardless of how tipsy you may be.

Istanbul's nightlife is certain to deliver, as long as you're up for the hangover. Rest assured that whichever continent side you end up in, with an open mind and wandering feet, a wild night is guaranteed.

Derya Bengi
Music journalist

I was the editor-in-chief of Roll magazine and contributed to *Express*, *Bir+Bir*, *Esquire*, *Cogito* and *Aktüel*. I curated an exhibition in 2012, dedicated to the 1960s Turkish music scene.

Arkaoda
P.091

Zeynep Erekli
Publishing director

I've worked as an editor in Time Out Istanbul and editor-at-large for Travel+Leisure Turkey. I've been working at Bone Magazine, a trend and travel monthly since 2012.

Engin Ayaz
Chief design officer

I take on architecture, industrial design and interface design projects, and is currently establishing creativity hub ATÖLYE Istanbul and teaching at Bilgi University's Architecture School.

Muaf
Beyoğlu
P.090

Barba
P.092

Uçman Balaban
Motion graphic designer

I specialise in motion graphics, animation and video. I studied visual communication design at İstanbul Bilgi University. I like to draw random pop culture junk in my spare time.

Zeplin
P.093

Peyote
Nevizade
P.094

Doğu Orcan
Editor in chief, Play Tuşu

I own more vinyl than I can listen to, way more liquor than I can drink and am religiously practicing Gonzo Journalism with the ardour of selfie-loving crossfitters and angry vegans.

Ali Kuru
Music producer

I have been DJ'ing and producing music for 15 years. I used to manage an Italian pizzeria in Beyoğlu, tries to stay on raw food and trains every day. I love solitude, DIY and small scale constructional stuff.

Geyik
P.095

Nejla Güvenç
Fashion designer, NEJ

Nejla Güvenç launched her own brand NEJ in 2001. She designs ecologic and organic clothing based on the materials used.

Anjelique
P.097

Merve Özaslan
Jewellery designer

Graduating from Mimar Sinan Fine Arts University, I'm a ceramic artist who designs jewellery and accessories. My work has been featured by British Vogue, Elle and Marie Claire.

Reha Öztunalı
Music producer

I'm a Rock 'n' roll lover, jazz seller, a "romantic" football fan and band manager who has been all around Europe and Istanbul's underground music scene for 10 years.

Zelda Zonk
P.096

COOP
P.098

Maksut Aşkar
Chef

I like to build a new way of looking into our traditions and childhood memories in Istanbul, and a way of understanding traditions is to give a crunchy edge to the viewers.

Salon İKSV
P.102

Cüneyt Cebenoyan
Actor

I'm also a film critic, radio programmer, DJ, economist, father, husband and Istanbulite.

Mercan Dede
Artist & musician

My name is Arkin, I create, produce and perform multimedia shows and visual art in many names. I consider myself extremely lucky and blessed to make my living by creating art.

Babylon
P.100

Volkswagen Arena
P.103

49 Muaf Beyoğlu
Map D, P.106

Seek refuge from crowds and cacophony of the pedestrian-only Istiklal Street by tucking into Muaf, located on one of its side streets. Following sudden fame during the Gezi Park protests, the bar had to close its doors temporarily. Upon reopening, the bar has served as an anti-establishment icon and often you'll meet guests who are in opposition to the current regime. Politics aside, the bar is cosy, intimate, and a breeding ground for alcohol induced wacky dance shows. Live music and DJ performances range from electro jazz and funk to soul, nu-disco and beyond.

🕙 1100–0300 (M-Th, Su), –0400 (F-Sa)
🏠 Şehit Muhtar, Kurabiye Sok. 4, Beyoğlu
📞 +90 212 243 2438   f Muaf Beyoğlu

"Visit *Gezi Park* as your 'after-party'. It's Istanbul's *Zuccotti Park, Tahrir* or *Plaza del Sol*."

– Derya Bengi

50 Arkaoda
Map I, P.109

Finding Arkaoda can come as a challenge with its discreet and unmarked door. But don't let that deter you from a good night out. Weekends are especially packed with the venue filling up with a diverse clientele so be ready for some close encounters. Curated by the owners of the city's best vinyl store Deform, the music is dynamic, ranging from reggae beats, indie tunes, electronica and house music. Although this is a nightlife spot, it's also a good place to grab an afternoon drink especially in its beautiful and spacious garden.

🕐 1200–0200 (M-Th, Su), –0300 (F–Sa)
🏠 Caferağa, Kadife Sok. 18A, Kadıköy
📞 +90 216 418 0277 ⓕ Arkaoda
🔗 www.arkaoda.com

"Arkaoda is unbeatably the best Kadıköy bar for independent music. Check for their 'strictly vinyl' nights of reggae and dub from the 70s to date."

– Zeynep Erekli, Bone Magazine

51 Barba

Map D, P.106

A proper pub is hard to come by in Istanbul. And Barba is just that – a cosy pub with a traditional horseshoe bar that allows strangers to mingle when ordering drinks. Local band Cümbüş Cemaat's musician Cem and his partners in crime bring together a cool crowd, fuelled by local and international beers that are hard to come by in many Istanbul bars. Live music most nights is a definite draw of this watering hole, adding ambience and good entertainment.

🕐 1700–0130 (M–Th), –0230 (F–Sa)
🏠 Halaskargazi, 2/F, Mis Sok. 6, Şişli
📞 +90 533 481 2313, +90 530 560 5287 ⓕ Barba

"Arrive early on weekends or visit during weekdays. It makes for a much nicer experience and a more intimate setting with less people there."

– Engin Ayaz, ATÖLYE Labs

 52 Zeplin
Map I, P.109

Whilst Istanbul's nightlife is known to be centred around Beyoğlu, it's worth the trek to Zeplin in Moda. It's a typical neighbourhood bar with an ultra hipster vibe that spills over to the sidewalk on most nights, especially on weekends, regardless of the weather. They have beers from Germany, Holland, Belgium, Mexico, England and beyond along with a whiskey selection that spans three pages of a menu. They've also got an extensive cocktail list with both classics and some Zeplin specialties. Typical bar food is also available like burgers and fries. They also have cider, which is quite rare for an Istanbul pub.

🕐 1100–0100 daily 🏠 Caferağa, Moda Cad. 70B, Kadıköy 📞 +90 216 700 2002 ⨍ Zeplin Pub

"It's like the Cheers bar in the TV series Cheers. Just grab a beer from the bar and stand outside. It's that kind of place."
– Uçman Balaban

53 Peyote Nevizade
Map D, P.106

Being approachable, affordable, and having a relaxed atmosphere, good vibes define this alternative concert venue where up-and-coming local bands and DJs take the stage on most nights, playing anything from jazz to Anatolian Rock. The best nights to visit are ones with live performances so be sure to check out the schedule of events before visiting. The terrace is great for having a beer and chatting in the open air. Try to arrive early on Fridays and Saturdays to make sure you get in.

🕐 1400-0400 daily
🏠 Hüseyinağa, Kameriye Sok. 4, Beyoğlu
📞 +90 212 251 4398 🅵 Peyote Nevizade
🆄🆁🅻 peyote.com.tr

"This is basically Istanbul's CBGB, making or breaking bands. Drinks are super cheap here. Get wasted and you might end the night like drunken David Hasselhoff."

– Doğu Orcan, Play Tuşu

54 Geyik

Map A, P.105

A coffee shop by day and cocktail bar by night, Geyik fulfills the drinking needs of the Cihangir area for locals and tourists alike. The bar takes up half of the space in this cosy, dark wood-clad venue which fills quickly, especially on the weekends. During the day, try the coffee which is roasted on site and sourced from different South American and African estates. At night, trust mixologist Yağmur Engin to make you something innovative like the Blackberry Cobbler, a mix of fruit and brandy or opt for a well-made classic, an Old Fashioned.

🕙 1000–0200 daily 🏠 Cihangir, Kilicali Pasa Mah.
Akarsu Cad. 22/A, Beyoğlu 📞 +90 532 773 0013
📘 Geyik Coffee Roastery & Cocktail Bar

"They make the best whisky sour."

– Ali Kuru

55 Zelda Zonk

Map A, P.104

A mixed crowd of 30-something celebs, so-cialites, hipsters, bloggers, and Karaköy locals head to Zelda Zonk around midnight when the tables are removed to make space for dancing. A huge crowd is common here as partiers pack the rooftop for its stunning views of the Old City, the Galata Bridge, and the Galata Tower. The resident DJ is Tarık Koray, who once moved the crowds in the now-lost legendary NuTeras, with a mix of Turkish and international pop and dance hits.

🕐 1900–0200 (M–Th), –0400 (F–Sa)
🏠 Bereketzade, Bankalar Cad. 2/1, Beyoğlu
📞 +90 530 382 3822   f Zelda Zonk

"It boasts an international vibe and a great view of the Golden Horn. It's one of my favourite nightlife spot for serious parties."

– Nejla Güvenç, NEJ

56 Anjelique
Map P, P.111

A classic of Istanbul's opulent nightlife scene, the two-storied, waterfront club is filled with all ages of Istanbul's elite. Dance to Turkish pop songs on one floor and house music on the other throwing your hands in the air. With the champagne flowing, be sure to wear your latest designer clothes to impress the crowd and fit in at this strictly posh locale. If a swanky night out isn't your thing, make a pitstop early in the evening just to grab a drink and enjoy the marvelous view.

🕐 1800-0400 daily (Apr 16-Dec), (Tu-Sa, Jan-Apr 15)
🏠 Ortaköy, Muallim Naci Cad., Salhane Sok. 5, Beşiktaş ☎ +90 212 327 2844 📘 Anjelique
🔗 www.anjelique.com.tr

"Don't miss this place in your trip. If weather permits, head to the terrace for its incredible view of the Bosporus bridge."

– Merve Özaslan

57 **COOP**
Map A, P.104

Live music performances as well as sets by local and international DJs turn COOP into a big party every week whether it be with funk, soul, rap, psychedelic, jazz, ska, or hiphop. Conveniently located on Istiklal Street, inside the Suriye Pasajı (a covered arcade), and spread over two floors, you may find yourself beating to different rhythms on the same night. It's a great spot to stop by to hear some tunes and drink a refreshing cocktail if you're out for a night of bar hopping around Beyoğlu.

🕓 2000–0200 (Tu–Th), –0400 (F–Sa)
🏠 Gümüşsuyu, İstiklal Cad., Suriye Pasajı 166/10, Beyoğlu   📞 +90 212 252 7181   f COOP Istanbul

"Ask to see if they have any 'wurst'! A limited sandwich they serve at the end of the night. Perfect match for your last beer."

– Reha Öztunalı, Tantana Records, Nublu İstanbul

58 Babylon
Map B, P.105

An iconic venue for live performance and music, Babylon has shaped Istanbul's music scene at its original venue in the Beyoğlu district for over a decade. It recently moved to Bomonti where the musical diversity continues to offer a wide array of performances, from local and international musicians playing anything from Ethiopian jazz and alternative rock to electronic and soul. Its beachside location is ideal, next to the festival area, a popular summer hangout. For a classic Babylon night, head to one of their monthly 'Oldies but Goldies' parties featuring tunes from decades past. Make sure to check their programme in advance and buy tickets for any event.

🕐 Showtime varies with programmes
🏠 Bomontiada: Tarihi Bomonti Bira Fabrikası, Birahane Sok. 1., Şişli, Kilyos: Kumköy, Demirci Köy Mevkii, Kilyos Yolu, Sarıyer
📞 +90 212 334 0190 🔗 babylon.com.tr

"This is one of the best spots in the city to listen to live bands."

– Maksut Aşkar

59 Salon İKSV
Map A, P.104

Home of the Istanbul Foundation for Culture and Arts - organisers of the Biennial and the Istanbul Music Festival, Film Festival and more - Salon is one of the most esteemed venues for good music in the city. This performance venue offers an eclectic mixture of genres and big names from Turkey and abroad, including indie-rock band St. Etienne, American jazz singer-songwriter Madeleine Peyroux, and alternative Turkish rock band Büyük Ev Ablukada. In addition to music, Salon hosts a number of panel discussions, literary events, workshops and theatre - something for every taste.

🕑 *Showtime varies with programmes*
🏠 *Şişhane, Nejat Eczacıbaşı Binası, Sadi Konuralp Cad. 5, Beyoğlu* 📞 *+90 212 334 0752*
URL *saloniksv.com*

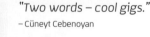

"Two words – cool gigs."
– Cüneyt Cebenoyan

60 Volkswagen Arena

Map R, P.111

Previously known as Black Box Istanbul, Volkswagen Arena is a massive multi-purpose venue with a capacity of 5,800 people, that hosts some of the biggest concerts, fashion shows and events in the city. State of the art acoustics and performances by world-renowned artists draw visitors to the arena as well as the 21 different food and drink outlets that help fuel the party. Located inside the UNIQ Istanbul cultural complex, the arena is in Maslak, and it's only a ten-minute walk from the ITU subway stop.

🕐 *Showtime varies with events*
🏠 *Huzur, Maslak Ayazağa Cad. 4A, Sarıyer*
📞 *+90 212 377 6700*   📘 *Volkswagen Arena*
🔗 *vwarena.com*

"Istanbul is big and traffic can be insane so take the subway to get there without hassle."

– Mercan Dede

DISTRICT MAP : BEYOĞLU, SARIYER

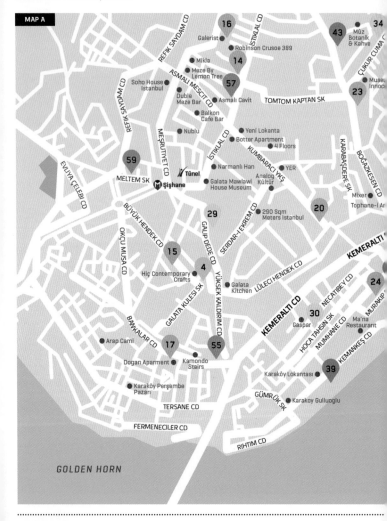

MAP A

- 16 Galerist
- Robinson Crusoe 389
- Mikla
- 14
- Meze By Lemon Tree
- 57
- Soho House Istanbul
- Duble Meze Bar
- Asmalı Cavit
- Balkon Cafe Bar
- Nublu
- Yeni Lokanta
- Botter Apartment
- 4 Floors
- Narmanlı Han
- YER
- Galata Mawlawi House Museum
- Analog Kültür
- Tünel
- Şişhane
- 29
- 290 Sqm Meters Istanbul
- 20
- Mixer
- Tophane-i Ar
- 15
- 4
- Hiç Contemporary Crafts
- Galata Kitchen
- 30
- Gaspar
- Ma'na Restaurant
- Arap Cami
- 17
- Kamondo Stairs
- 55
- Karaköy Lokantası
- 39
- Dogan Aparment
- Karaköy Perşembe Pazarı
- Karakoy Gulluoglu
- 24
- 43
- Müz Botanik & Kahve
- 34
- Muse Innoc
- 23

REFIK SAYDAM CD
İSTİKLAL CD
ASMALI MESCIT CD
TOMTOM KAPTAN SK
REFIK SAYDAM CD
MEŞRUTIYET CD
İSTİKLAL CD
KUMBARACI YKŞ
KARABAŞDERE SK
BOĞAZKESEN CD
EVLIYA ÇELEBI CD
MELTEM SK
59
BÜYÜK HENDEK CD
GALIP DEDE CD
SERDAR-I EKREM CD
OKÇU MUSA CD
GALATA KULESI SK
LÜLECI HENDEK CD
KEMERALTI
YÜKSEK KALDIRIM CD
KEMERALTI CD
NECATIBEY CD
BANKALAR CD
HOCA TAHSIN SK
MUMHANE CD
MURAKIP
KEMANKEŞ CD
GÜMRÜK SK
TERSANE CD
FERMENECILER CD
RIHTIM CD
CUKUR CUMA
EVLIYA ÇELEBI CD

GOLDEN HORN

- 34_Çukurcuma
- 39_Gümrük
- 41_Akali
- 42_Journey
- 43_Münferit
- 45_Dandin Bakery
- 54_Geyik
- 55_Zelda Zonk
- 57_COOP
- 58_Babylon
- 59_Salon İKSV

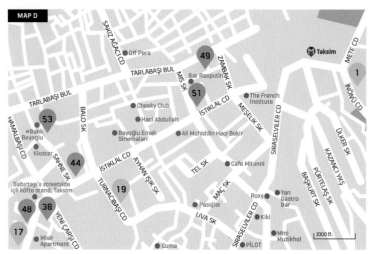

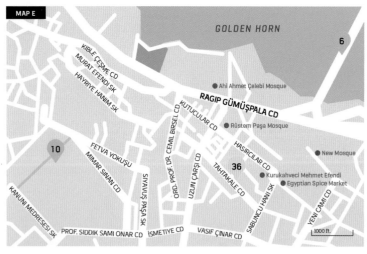

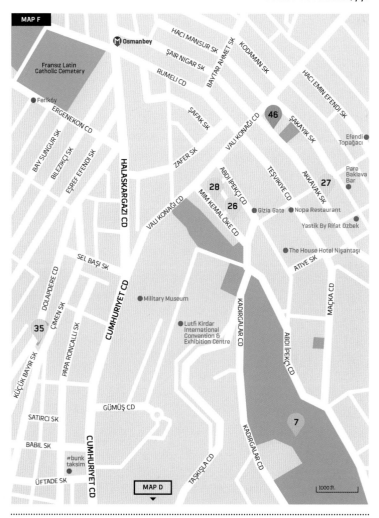

- ● 7_Maçka Demokrasi Parkı
- ● 26_Shopi go No:17
- ● 27_ECNP Gallery
- ● 28_FEY
- ● 35_Dolapdere Bit Pazarı
- ● 46_Kantin

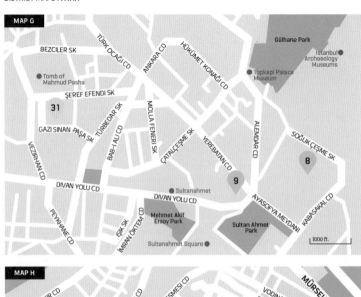

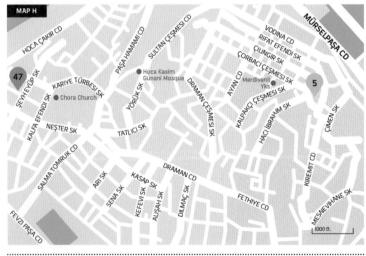

- 5_Balat
- 8_Ayasofya
- 9_Yerebatan Sarayı
- 31_Abdulla @Kapalı Çarşı
- 47_Asitane Restaurant

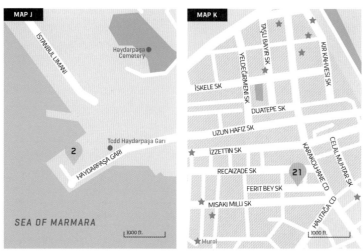

DISTRICT MAPS : **EYÜP, KADIKÖY, SARIYER**

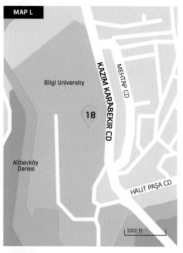

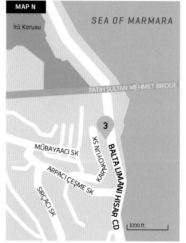

- 3_Perili Köşk
- 12_Caddebostan Konak
- 18_santralistanbul
- 22_Sakıp Sabancı Müzesi

- ● 11_Kanyon
- ◐ 25_Sanayi 313
- ● 56_Anjelique
- ● 60_Volkswagen Arena

Accommodation

Hip hostels, fully-equipped apartments & swanky hotels

No journey is perfect without a good night's sleep to recharge. Whether you're backpacking or on a business trip, our picks combine top quality and convenience, whatever your budget.

💲 <240 TL 💲 241–735 TL 💲 736 TL+

4 Floors İstanbul

Take in both Turks' love for crafts and modern lifestyle here. Close to all local amenities in a quiet location, this 19th-century terraced building offers four lofty apartments, one on each floor. Each unit boasts designer fixtures from owner Sema Topaloğlu's own firm and a fully-equipped kitchen but the penthouse has a rooftop terrace and the best views of the Sea of Marmara.

🏠 Tomtom Mah., Tercuman Cikmazi 20, Beyoğlu 💲
📞 +90 532 497 7921 🔗 4floorsistanbul.com 💲

Stories Rooms Galata

Trendy cafés, galleries and important landmarks won't be far from the footsteps of this boutique residence. Bulent Gungor, who masterfully restored Yıldız Palace, fitted the historic building with his sleek furniture designs. Selected rooms feature kitchenettes and private terraces. Stories also own three other hotels in Taksim.

🏠 Sahkulu, Kumbaraci Yokusus 37, Beyoğlu
📞 +90 212 293 3186 **URL** storiesroomsgalata.com 💲

#bunk Taksim

Housed in a historic building, #bunk Taksim is a
hostel that offers a boutique hotel experience.
Neat and functionally designed for a conve-
nient stay, it is situated in a quiet neighbourhood five minutes away from Taksim Square's
hustle and bustle. Solo travellers will appreciate
the spacious electronic lockers in each room.

🏠 İnönü, Papa Roncalli Sok. 34, Şişli
☎ +90 212 343 0095 URL bunkhostels.com

Room Mate Kerem

🏠 Kamer Hatun,
Meşrutiyet Cad. 34, Beyoğlu
📞 +90 212 245 0245
URL kerem.room-matehotels.com

Taksim 15

🏠 Gümüşsuyu, İnönü Cad. 15, Beyoğlu
📞 +90 212 243 1367
URL taksim15.com

The House Hotel Nişantaşı

🏠 Nişantaşı, Abdi İpekçi Cad. 34, Şişli
📞 +90 212 224 5999
🌐 www.thehousehotel.com/
the-house-hotel-nisantasi.aspx

Istanbul! Place Apartments

🏠 Multiple locations in central Galata
📞 +90 545 435 7057
🌐 istanbulplace.com

Notes

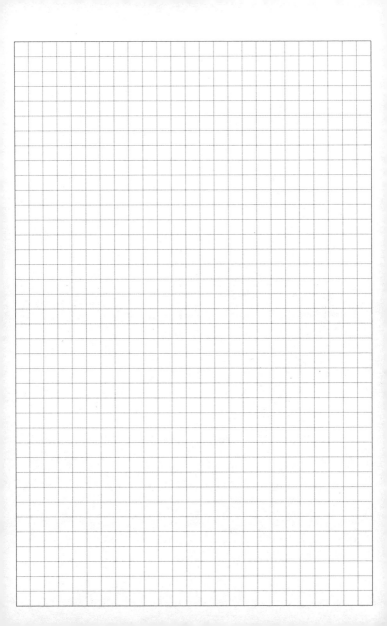

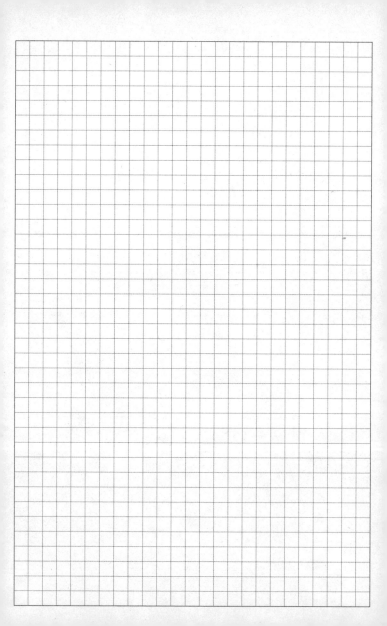

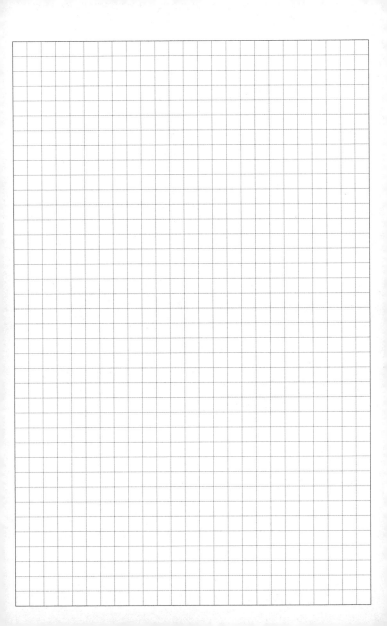

Index

Media & Publishing

Aylin Güngör
@Bant Magazine, p067
www.bantmag.com,
gingerandoak.tumblr.com

Doğu Orcan @Play Tuşu, p094
www.playtusu.com,
www.zombikreatif.com

Hande Oynar @Luxos, p060
www.luxos.com

Hazal Yılmaz, p079
hazalyilmaz.com,
cokgezenlerkulubu.com

James Hakan Dedeoğlu
@Bant Magazine, p076
www.bantmag.com,
tsuman.bandcamp.com

Zeynep Erekli
@Bone Magazine, p091
www.bonemagazine.com

Multimedia

Can Büyükberber, p016
www.canbuyukberber.com

Tamer Nakışçı
@Futureisblank, p028
www.tamernakisci.com,
www.futureisblank.com

Uçman Balaban, p093
www.ucmanbalaban.com

Music

Ahmet Uluğ @Pozitif, p063
www.pozitiflive.com
Portrait by muhsin

Ali Kuru, p095
alikuru.info

Alican Tezer , p048
instagram.com/alicantezer

Derya Bengi, p090

Dilara Karolina Sakpınar, p039
www.123theband.com,

www.laradilara.com, sound-
cloud.com/alikeplaces

Melis Danişmend, p049
www.melisdanismend.com.tr

Mercan Dede, p103
www.mercandede.com,
instagram.com/mercandede

Murat Beşer, p020
www.muratbeser.com

Reha Öztunalı
@Tantana Records,
Nublu İstanbul, p098
tantanarecords.com,
nubluistanbul.net

Photography

Can Dağarslanı, p082
www.candagarslani.com

Coşkun Aşar, p074
facebook.com/coskun.asar

Eylül Aslan, p062
www.septemberlion.com

Muhsin Akgün, p064
www.muhsinakgun.com

Tanla Özuzun, p047
www.tanlaozuzun-fa.blogspot.
com, www.1000atli.net

Photo & other credits

Anjelique, p097
(All) Ali Bekman, Merve Hasman

Arter, p036–037
(p036 Top & p037 middle left)
Serkan Taycan
(p036 Bottom) Aras Selim
Bankoglu
(p037 Top & bottom left) Murat
Germen (Bottom right) Hadiye
Cangokce

Asitane Restaurant, p084
(All) Asitane Restaurant

Ayasofya, p024–025
(p025) Jorge Láscar on Flickr

Babylon, p100–101
(p100 Bottom & p101) Kali Pro

COOP, p098–099
(All) Yunus Dölen, Uygar Taylan

Galata Kulesi, p017–019
(p017 Bottom) Abdulaziz Ceylan
on Flickr

Istanbul Modern, p034–035
(p034) Sahir Uğur Eren, Muhsin
Akgün

Perili Köşk, p016
(p010 & p016 Bottom) Hadiye
Cangökçe (Middle) Andrew Rog-
ers Cözülen Unfurling - 2007

Peyote Nevizade, p094
(p086, p094 Top & middle) Barış
Elif Flufoto

Salon İKSV, p102
(Top & middle) Ali Güler

Sakıp Sabancı Müzesi, p047
(All) Murat Germen

Sanayi 313, p054–055
(All) Ersen Çörekçi

Volkswagen Arena, p103
(All) Kali Pro

–
In Accommodation: all courtesy
of respective hotels.

CITIX60

CITIx60: Istanbul

First published and distributed by
viction workshop ltd

viction:ary™

7C Seabright Plaza, 9-23 Shell Street,
North Point, Hong Kong

Url: www.victionary.com
Email: we@victionary.com
🅵 www.facebook.com/victionworkshop
🐦 www.twitter.com/victionary_
🐙 www.weibo.com/victionary

Edited and produced by viction:ary

Concept & art direction: Victor Cheung
Research & editorial: Queenie Ho, Caroline Kong
Project coordination: Jovan Lip, Katherine Wong
Design & map illustration: MW Wong, Frank Lo, Bryan Leung

Co-curator & contributing project coordinator: C. Efe Öç
Contributing writer: Talya Arditi
Contributing editor: Katee Hui
Cover map illustration: Beril Ateş
Count to 10 illustrations: Guillaume Kashima aka Funny Fun
Photography: Tuncay Dersinlioglu

Content is compiled based on facts available as of January 2016. Travellers
are advised to check for updates from respective locations before your visit.

First edition
ISBN 978-988-13204-8-3
Printed and bound in China

Acknowledgements

A special thank you to all creatives, photographer(s), editor, producers, companies and organisations for your crucial contributions to our inspiration and
knowledge necessary for the creation of this book. And, to the many whose
names are not credited but have participated in the completion of the book,
we thank you for your input and continuous support all along.

CITIX60

City Guides

CITIx60 is a handpicked list of hot spots that illustrates the spirit of the world's most exhilarating design hubs. From what you see to where you stay, this city guide series leads you to experience the best — the places that only passionate insiders know and go.

Each volume is a unique collaboration with local creatives from selected cities. Known for their accomplishments in fields as varied as advertising, architecture and graphics, fashion, industry and food, music and publishing, these locals are at the cutting edge of what's on and when. Whether it's a one-day stopover or a longer trip, **CITIx60** is your inspirational guide.

Stay tuned for new editions.

City guides available now:

Amsterdam
Barcelona
Berlin
Copenhagen
Hong Kong
Istanbul
London
Los Angeles
Melbourne
New York
Paris
Portland
Stockholm
Tokyo
Vienna